I Don't Know Why She was Proud of Me

William Brown

McClure Publishing, Inc.

Copyright © 2023
William Brown for McClure Publishing, Inc.

All rights reserved. Printed and bound in the United States of America. According to the 1976 United States Copyright Act, no part of this book may be reproduced or utilized in any form or by any means, electronic or mechanical, including photocopying, recording, or by any information storage or retrieval system, except by a reviewer who may quote brief passages in a review to be printed in a magazine or newspaper, without permission in writing from the Publisher: Inquiries should be addressed to McClure Publishing, Inc. Permissions Department, 398 West Army Trail Road, Bloomingdale, IL 60108. First Printing: July 4, 2023.

ISBN-13: 979-8-9877802-1-3

To order additional copies, please contact:

McClure Publishing, Inc.
https://McClurePublishing.com
800.659.4908

This book is dedicated to all those who have lost loved one(s) due to different forms of cancer.

~ and ~

Written for my grandchildren who loved you, Mommy, before they were born.

INTRODUCTION

At times I feel lost without Mother not being alive anymore. I feel like I'm in an alternate universe, and I need to get back to my reality.

Mother enjoyed life and was a warmhearted lady. She suffered during her last days before she died from ovarian cancer. She always practiced preventive medicine getting her flu shot every year and was fully vaccinated and boosted.

I feel like I didn't show up when she needed me the most, although, I was by her side in those last moments.

She was my friend. We watched movies together and took walks and had one-on-one talks. She gave me sound advice from a woman's point of view, and she was fair.

When she would get jovial, she rejoiced with an unforgettable smile. Her face would be full of delight.

She tried her best to prepare for what was happening to her. The stage four cancer moved throughout her body quickly each day draining her strength.

It seemed as if her body was betraying her. Although, her will to live was much stronger. Eventually, she had to surrender to the disease.

I'm *gonna* miss cooking her breakfast and dinner while watching her eat and enjoying it.

I'm *gonna* miss hearing her fingers snapping and grooving to the music she loved.

I'm *gonna* miss her requesting to make the yellow rice with olives in it saying it was yummy.

I'm *gonna* miss her generosity and her aggression when I may not have paid her back on time. She was a Harlem lady with a lot of gangster mannerisms as she reprimanded me.

I'm *gonna* miss the way we'd listened to new music together, and she'd asked, "Billy who sing that record?" and I'd reply so and so, and she'd say, "I like that record."

And most of all I'm *gonna* miss her saying, "Love you, Billy."

I Don't Know Why She Was Proud Of Me

"I Don't Know why She was Proud of Me." Thoughts run through my mind, *what had I done for her overall?* I couldn't save her. I felt defeated. Nothing I could have done or said would have saved her.

Maybe I should've called the ambulance sooner. I probably didn't make the right decision with her diet, or maybe I wasn't connecting with her enough during her last year on this earth. Not getting awfully close to her as I should've. Even when I did spend time with her, I felt like she was far away.

We had forty-nine years on this planet together. Did we really know one another? I keep thinking that I may have not utilized every second we were awarded together to make our relationship stronger.

She watched me as I lived my life. I watched her throughout the decades. I even looked up to her, my mind was so impressionable, due to the lack of a strong father figure in our home.

In my community a lot of mothers raised their sons on their own. My Mother was my role model. I wanted to be a secretary and type as fast as she did. She had an old typewriter with a ribbon inside of it and a carriage return. It was built like a tank and very heavy when I tried to lift it. I can remember the sounds it made when the type bars struck the paper, she loaded it manually page after page typing at 100 wpm.

I wanted no drama. I just wanted to sing our songs and have our precious moments growing old together.

I Don't Know Why
She Was Proud Of Me

Maybe we could have the blessings of her seeing me become a grandfather and she a great-grandmother.

I knew death is a reality we all must face. Why did I think with all the tragic events going on around us throughout the years, death wouldn't come knocking on our door one day?

It's hard to come to terms with the feeling I didn't do everything I possibly could to extend her lifespan. I was right there along with my wife; we both were caught unexpectedly. We were actually looking forward to her being cancer free.

There were many ups and downs on this emotional rollercoaster, but one thing I knew when I read between the lines of what the doctors were telling me was for certain Mommy was going to die from this disease.

The palliative care doctor kept me informed at all times of the day while doctors and students carried on with their numerous patients on schedule.

I spoke to some of the nurses and explained to them to be gentle inserting needles and devices into her arms because her veins were hard to reach, and it would be torture for her by continuously sticking needles in her skin.

My Mother called them the vampires and she fought them every time. Nurses changed shifts from the day to night. The night shift nurse was in charge of taking her blood. She gave off vibes that she was only there to do her shift. I let my presence be known as did her granddaughters, Auntie Cheryl, and my wife Eurdise.

She looked at me through the iPhone that the palliative care nurse held. I was thankful that the nurse showed me so much professionalism and concern.

The palliative care nurse walks with a cane and she reminds me of the character Dr. Gregory House.

Sometimes it felt like I was in an episode of "House." House was a television show that came on ABC Thursday nights. The show was about a male head physician in a teaching school in New Jersey. He had ingenious and clever ways to make his patients feel confident and would assure them that they were in the best care.

Each episode during the intro you would see him walking down the corridor talking amongst his colleagues. My reality was seeing this woman walk down the hall of the cancer unit talking with my Mother's primary physician.

She bathed Mom and applied lotion on her keeping her skin soft and smooth. I could tell she was really being cared for by this woman. She was a special person who held her hand and talked to Mommy throughout the day.

My Mother had made another friend. One of the last people to bond with her. I still keep in touch with her today. Her name is Patricia.

Her eyes called out to me. It was the clearest visual of my Mother through the phone. It was as if she had makeup on. Her hair started growing back too. She was crystal clear as I viewed her on FaceTime. I could tell she was uncomfortable, still frustrated and maybe feeling a little pain.

"Billy, I need you!!!" Her big wide eyes spoke to me, connecting to my inner child. As I looked into her eyes, they spoke as if she was telling me to get something for her or explaining something profoundly serious to me. I would not ignore this sign. I had to listen. She was taking her last breaths. We were up to the point of her life that at any day and any moment she could have passed.

She didn't want to die. Her eyes told me it's her time. *I don't want to die like this, but if I have to, I need you by my side.* She had missed the holiday season, and I don't think she knew what time or day it was, but this wasn't a good day to die. She wanted to live.

"I can't fight no more Billy this thing is killing me." As her eyes conversed with me in a short amount of time.

She grew tired of the treatments and not getting better made her feel let down, along with the physical therapy. The doctors suggested she should do it.

She fought in her own way and would tell me how much she exercised by walking around the island in the kitchen, as she depended on her walker for stability back and forth to the bathroom.

We spoke about her condition and her survival rate dealing with this disease often on our car rides to receive treatment. I would look at her in the passenger side of the car while I drove her to wherever she needed to go.

She enjoyed going shopping in various stores, the market, and little bargain clothing stores with my wife, her daughter.

Their relationship was more than the usual mother-in-law and daughter-in-law as her health would start to get complex and her medicines changed.

My mom felt special when they'd go to Walgreens to get her prescriptions filled. I would say things to make her laugh, and to encourage her that there was hope for her, and that we were working together with the doctors to help her through this ordeal.

We spoke about her attempting to eat more, drinking her water, and the exercises the physical therapist told her to do which would strengthen her muscles.

She listened to other cancer victims give their testimony on how they were fighting cancer and she wished them well and prayed for them. But her fight had taken its toll on her mentally and physically.

Financially, she had great medical coverage which secured her stay and medicines, some were awfully expensive, one pill can be more than fifty dollars.

She could not verbalize anything; her eyes were the window to her soul.… Helplessly drifting into the unknown. Her eyes looked like a child asking for help while trapped in an adult world with no clue where to turn or who to listen to. But God was calling and getting her ready. She wanted to speak to me, but she couldn't.

I was conflicted and saddened about the constant treatments, these treatments made her loopy as she would say, then at other times she would have a surge of energy like her old self. Then there were times when she felt totally crappy when taking her pain meds.

While we were making her chemo appointments on time and never late, traveling to the hospital with her walker, she called it a Cadillac. She did not have nauseating experiences till Christmas Eve.

She hardly complained about pain until now, and if she did, it wasn't to this degree where pain medication would be given to her every four to five hours or as much as she needed.

I still left my workplace like clockwork to support and care for her. I used my sick time, vacation time, and I was gifted time as well by my Director of Operations.

My Mom had a device inserted down her throat to relieve her from the constant vomiting. It was the main piece of medical equipment that prevented her from speaking without feeling pain. It was also unpleasant to see.

The tube was used to suction the greenish brownish fluid that was involuntarily exiting her body. It was bile. The fluid flowed through a tube that was connected to a canister where you can see the measurements of the fluid being collected by the ounce.

She received nourishment through those other tubes and intravenous connections. There was a bag with a milky substance, and then there were other bags connected which were there to keep her hydrated, and also ones that distributed pain medication.

I watched the heart monitor and the blood pressure readouts, and alerted the nursing staff when the sensor went off. The sound of the heart monitor beeping is still in my head.

She hadn't eaten anything solid for the remainder of the five weeks of her life. She hadn't eaten a lot the way she used to anyway. Her appetite was probably a nibble here and a swallow of water or a sip here and there.

She didn't like the ensure protein shakes, so we made shakes for her. We also cooked egg whites and toast as well as offered her Gatorade®.

I remember I shouted at her out of frustration one afternoon because she was not eating anything. I told her I wanted her to live more than she wanted to live, and she started to cry.

I was being selfish and a spoiled brat, I wanted things to go my way and not considering what she was going through and how tough it was living through the cancer.

She later explained to me, as I apologized to her. She just didn't have the will to eat but she was trying. She was a petite woman who was already small, so with the hospital gown on and the covers over her, it was hard to tell how small she really had gotten.

She was throwing up more than twenty-five times a day. I counted. It was amazing how much stomach fluid your body produces to digest your food. She didn't have any food to digest, but she continuously threw up. I know that her esophagus was sore because of it and that was another thing that halted her speech too.

I had them take the device out of her throat because it frustrated her and made her extremely uncomfortable. Who could live comfortably with a device connected to your face and a device inserted down your throat. She was already in a lot of pain. And from all that I observed, she needed less suffering and more time to relax.

Was her body working hard to heal or was her body preparing to shut down? These were the uncertainties I would have to face, while there were days where it seemed she would be doing better than other times.

The doctors and palliative care specialists told me this is natural during transitioning. She would succumb to her illness shortly and definitely would not live to see her 71st birthday which was in March.

We were nearing the end of January. I can remember when I asked her doctor at one time in December, "Would she make it to the new year?"

He answered with, "The Lord has the last say. We are doing everything we can to make her comfortable."

They put her on a medicine that would suppress the vomiting but made her look Zombified. I spoke to the doctors on the phone, and they explained to me about this powerful drug they would administer. It would make her super drowsy and unaware of her surroundings.

It would suppress the vomiting and end the pain. My Mother was in constant pain and vomiting around the clock. So, I agreed to go ahead with it.

"Yes, give it to her she needs relief from her body working hard because at this point, we were beyond healing. We needed a miracle and mercy."

After a while of being on the medicine, I had to make a choice, either she'd stay on that medicine which left her vulnerable, and totally out of it. In addition, she wouldn't even notice who came to visit her, especially me.

I couldn't agree with that any longer, because when I came to visit her the next day, she looked like she wasn't alive.

I would look at her chest to see if she was breathing, I saw her chest moving in and out. I took her pulse to make sure she was alive, but her appearance was not acceptable.

So, I told them not to give her that medication anymore. I'd rather them give her the medicine that relieved her pain, but the vomiting would continue. At least she would have some control of her body, and she would notice loved ones and myself coming to visit her.

The nursing staff, my Mommy, and I would wipe the spew from her mouth each time she vomited. This was a lot sometimes when the bile would spill on her gown, and I would ask the nurse could she change it please.

I propped her head beside a pillow so if the nursing staff weren't available the substance would flow onto a napkin which was also propped below the pillow.

She was still strong. She was still taking care of herself. I know she was during those moments when it was just her alone in the room. The palliative nurse told me about her alertness, and she had to maintain her beautiful appearance. She ate as much ice chips as she could, and I also used Vaseline® to keep her lips from chapping.

She was still fighting like she promised me she would. When we talked, she sounded doubtful like if you had to fight a bully and you know it's a possibility you could win but then it's a big chance you may lose.

She was fearless but this was something she had no control over. She had all faith in God because man had failed her so many times before as I sat by her bedside till the visiting hours were over. I wanted to stay but due to COVID restrictions I had to leave.

There were doctors and nurses running in and out of her room. Some making their rounds, some taking her temperature and vital signs, and then there was the cleaning crew who did an excellent job of maintaining her room's appearance by mopping, sweeping, and wiping.

My wife and I would take turns visiting. Only one person could visit each day. I would visit mostly because I worked in Baltimore, and I was fifteen to twenty minutes from the hospital or hospice. My wife would come on Fridays and sometimes in the middle of the week and on weekends we'd alternate.

Every time we visited, we felt defeated, but we had to make sure our mom knew she was not alone. We had to stay on top of the nursing staff.

There are rumors that when your loved ones that's hospitalized don't have people that come to see them regularly, they get cared for less. We did not want that to occur. We needed all the attention and care her health benefits covered.

Due to pandemic restrictions, there was extremely limited visits. So, when the grands did visit, they had to visit one at a time per day. I wanted to see her every day, but I could not be selfish.

We wore masks when we entered and washed our hands several times and was careful not to touch a lot of things. One time, they had to move her to a different floor because someone tested positive for COVID. Fortunately for my Mother, she didn't test positive.

We were making sure she could hear us say words of encouragement, so we talked to her about current events and reminded her of all the love and support she has. I also held her hand and squeezed it enough to see if I got a squeeze back. Her squeezes back got weaker by the day, but I was sensitive to her touch. I believe she knew it was me. Her hair was so soft as I ran my fingers through it.

We had her communicate with the outside world via FaceTime, but not as much now as we did before. I know she wouldn't want to let people see her on one of her bad days and most of the time she was out of it. In between those in and out moments, I would try to keep her awake before she dozed off because of the heavy pain medication that was given to her.

We'd even have her listen to audio from her friends, who called on her cellphone. Her friends loved to speak words of encouragement over the phone to her before she was admitted to the hospital or hospice.

My wife and brother-in-law's mother, who had cancer too spoke with her daily. They encouraged one another. They had the same procedures and they comforted one another through this disease. My Mother's disease got more aggressive than hers and Mom could no longer engage in conversation or text with her daily. They were the Prayer Warrior Sisters.

Prayer warriors, loved ones, and the whole congregation from her church sent words filled with love, text messages, cards through snail mail, and devotionals. Many showed affection towards my wife and I during this time. They felt what we were doing was taking a toll on us too.

There's a saying if you go to jail your family does the time with you. Well, if your loved one is hospitalized you feel ill too with hopelessness and loss for words just enough strength to show more support and drive to pull through.

She was tired and frustrated of dealing with the doctors who told her they would attempt to remove the cancer by agreeing to have a full hysterectomy and only to hear that the cancer had spread.

She was tired of feeling weak then strong then an awful crash spiraling. She had gotten frustrated with looking forward and seeing how much work it took to only have her sickness labeled TERMINAL. At one point, she was fighting for her quality of life. Now she's just tired.

All medicinal strategies, surgeries, and techniques were performed but was not making her better. They inserted a bridge in her bile duct that didn't work. The removal of all her lady parts didn't help. The radiation chemo and physical therapy didn't work.

One time the prayer warriors said prayers for one of my friends to cure him from stomach cancer. The prayers didn't work either. He died. I became discouraged. I had to realize prayer always work.

I Don't Know Why She Was Proud Of Me

My emotions were everywhere. I was not thinking clearly. I was an only child wanting my way, I wanted my Mother to live. I looked at other older women around her age and felt sad. I looked at others who drank and smoked regularly. I felt life wasn't fair. She had been clean for over ten years. She began her relationship with God. My life was not smooth, it was on rocky terrain.

I took my frustrations and anger out on my supervisor and manager at work. I knew I was wrong as I looked back. I felt a rage that I knew I could control but I didn't.

I accused them of micromanaging and overlooking my contributions to the company. No one built up moral and linked them to legal inner hustles internally like me. I made them stacks to put in their pockets during the vaccinated/unvaccinated season. How dare they?

I lost my cool, or was I really myself? Yes and No. My mind and body weren't there, my soul was with her.

I loved holding her hand. I looked at her nails, stared into her palms, and rubbed her hand on my face. I could feel her eyes following me as I prepared the sofa in order to stretch out overnight sometimes. I didn't know if she was proud of me when I left her alone in that hospital room with the television on.

My oldest two daughters are healthcare providers and nurses as well. They were highly concerned about their grandma. My daughters did research and found procedures that may have worked if my Mother's body wasn't shutting down.

I Don't Know Why
She Was proud Of Me

They got a chance to talk to her, bathe her, put lotion on her, and pray with her. They also witnessed the uncontrollable vomiting, and the exhaustion my Mother's body was experiencing. They had just lost their maternal grandparents the previous year.

Their sisterhood would be struck with the blow of death once more to share with their other siblings. They had input on treatments, they spoke with the head nurse and palliative care nurses and were present in meetings with her doctors via iPhone.

They were terribly busy in the New York City healthcare system. The pandemic restrictions had not yet dropped its code from Red. A few months later, it dropped to color yellow.

They would also speak with her by FaceTime, especially when she had the strength to smile or wave hello.

I would have all three of her granddaughters and her grandsons talk with her. My son visited her. It was tough on him. He still cries till this day. They were close and they were neighbors within our home.

My Mother was fair with all her grands, that's why her granddaughter drove six hours in total to visit, sit, watch movies, eat, and go out to dinner with her.

It's always a surprising delight to see the safe passage they would get; and the joy in grandma's eyes when they knocked on her door, and she granted them entry.

I Don't Know Why She Was Proud Of Me

The oldest is her first granddaughter Nachelle Monique Brown. She'd come through with her dog "Navy" a Pomeranian. That dog would make my Mother smile and chuckle in her own natural girlie way. She was a dog lover. We had a dog before his name was "Hannibal" that's a while back and I don't know what happened to him. I do know I couldn't take care of him, but like I said "Navy" Mom thought he was the cutest.

Regularly they'd be coming from upstate New York and Yonkers New York. Her and her Sister, April Renai Brown. These are the moments I share in memoriam. This was the time to let her know you were there for her.

This was my Mother, but let's not forget the others who have lost their mothers too. They would post their mother's pictures on their Facebook feed. I had a lot of support through this painful event, from people who've lost their mothers. I never knew the pain of being on standby at your mother's bedside as she is dying. This was strange to me.

I was on my way to Stella Maris Hospice; my mind was racing with great concern. I recall weaving in and out of traffic through the narrow backroads in silence. Just my thought process on her pain level. Maybe this was the last time I would be visiting her. This frustrated me. It left me feeling powerless. I thought I had prepared myself for my greatest loss.

I Don't Know Why She Was proud Of Me

The ride there from my place of work made me want to drive slowly. I didn't want this to be the day I had to say goodbye to my Mother.

I barely revved the engine. I was driving at a snail's pace as my Kia Optima Sedan purred, all I could do was think about her.

Along the route I signaled three rights, and a left lane signal going slowly down the curvy road with speed bumps ahead.

I was making time to collect my emotions, so I don't burst into tears in front of Mommy, and then there were times; I'd drive really fast, because I didn't want to get there and find out she passed on my way to her. This happened to me before when I planned on seeing my Father in a hospital in Harlem. He got sick and passed away very quickly while I was on my way to see him.

I've never detected any intravenous drug usage about him, but I knew he had lots of women. My Father didn't get riddled with bullets on the streets either. I'll share with you more about him later.

While driving I'd sometimes play songs that she would've enjoyed listening too. Then I would start sobbing into a full outburst of emotional tears. It got too painful listening to the music she loved.

The roads were opened wide most of the time especially on the weekends with the exception of traffic lights, evening construction, potholes, squeegee boys, and panhandlers in the middle of the street.

My head had to be clear. I needed to focus on my driving, because I didn't know what could pop out on the roads. I had never taken this route before. I was a New Yorker driving in Baltimore, Maryland.

The GPS was my partner. I had to be alert during daytime, and nighttime driving; because a family of deer, foxes, squirrels, or people could cross the road at any given time. I didn't have time for any of it, no speeding tickets, car breakdowns, accidents, or anything.

I really needed a safe passage from point A to point B, every second mattered. The days that my mom and I would take for granted and live through were now an uphill battle to get to.

You had your start of the week and then you get to Wednesday some people call it "Humpday" because it can be a struggle making it to the middle of the week, and by the time you get to Thursday, you coast on the good vibe that the weekend is near we called Thursday Friday Eve.

We looked forward to Fridays. Especially people in the workforce. Friday is the gateway to a three-day weekend when you combine it with a vacation day. A chance at getting ready to have no concern for the next workday, because you have a couple of days for yourself. Some people greet each other by saying, "Happy Friday," besides the normal greeting, "Good morning."

I Don't Know Why
She Was proud Of Me

My Mother loved saying "Happy Friday" when this time of the week had been reached. That is a wonderful thing to say to start the day after a long arduous work week.

My Mother had an album called "Thank God it's Friday," and she would play the title track often as I looked at its album artwork song credits and all. I was raised to appreciate this day for what it was at an incredibly youthful age.

Saturday was always to me the most American thing since James Brown and HipHop. The television schedule changed, and soap operas didn't come on. There would be cookouts, block parties, festivals, and jams that occurred Saturday afternoons in all neighborhoods within the five boroughs of New York City.

The nightclubs, whether hole in the wall or big disco tech clubs felt that Saturday night energy.

There was a movie titled "Saturday Night Fever" starring John Travolta. The soundtrack was recorded by The BEE GEES. That energy spilled over onto Mommy. She had that album and played it on the weekends. I used to hold it and gaze at the artwork and its song credits as well.

Saturdays are fulfilling, and welcoming. A continuous blessing, of merciful nighttime action, being up and about. Wherever you are, especially in the New York City nightlife.

I Don't Know Why She Was Proud Of Me

Saturday is a whole different vibe, and many of times my Mother let me know, by her actions. Today is a good day to clean your house and play music.

We interacted very well with each other on Saturdays. It seemed as if the sun shines the best on Saturdays, as I continued to reflect on the precious seconds we shared.

We needed mercy from God to end all pain she was going through. I was unprepared for this hurt, Lord. Oh, merciful one, we pray in your holy name, amen. A miracle needed to appear for us.

Seventy years old is a great age to reach. I've noticed women in their 70s well and fit. I wish she was in top physical shape. I admire the families that I see taking care of their female elders on my daily walks and time spent on the internet.

My Mother was ready to see a miracle, because she knew Jesus is a healer and a provider. She had witnessed it, and she believed in miracles. It was a miracle she lived to see everything throughout a rewarding 70-year lifespan.

I was ready to witness another miracle. I witnessed babies coming through the birth canal, knowing the risk a mother takes with her own life bearing children.

We've heard that miracles happen every day and people pull through, could this be another miracle I can witness too. I will always have patience for miracles to happen. One more second is a miracle. I thank you Lord for those miraculous moments.

I Don't Know Why
She Was Proud Of Me

I had been going to the hospice like clockwork. Hospice is basically the final moments you and your loved ones have to spend with one another.

There were other families there, at the Hospice Facility. I noticed them caring for their loved ones at this final stage of their journey.

I had become sensitive; my senses were heightened. I could hear residents breathing. I could sense the sorrow. I could feel their compassion. I could also feel the strength of a will to live but the burden of death was too great.

The nurses worked with their patients until their shifts were over, you hardly noticed them coming and going. It was quite somber inside. The hospice was quiet. I've been coming to this place every day since mom was transported from Baltimore General Hospital. While driving home, I would be half asleep and would catch myself before I dosed off.

It was a facility on a campus deep within the beautiful state of Maryland home of the current face of Boxing Gervontae "Tank" Davis, NBA Star Kevin Durant, Songstress Toni Braxton, academy award winning actor Mo'Nique, and The Great Bambino Babe Ruth. When I entered the locked doors, there was a long wide corridor with porcelain colored carpeted flooring. Its width had space enough for stretchers to be used.

There was a security desk with officers changing shifts assisting you with the sign-in/sign-out sheets.

I Don't Know Why She Was Proud Of Me

A full chapel on the left-hand side of the extensive hallway where priest would hold services and talk with families.

They had a Memorial Service in remembrance of The Late Reverend Dr Martin Luther King Junior in mid-January.

I got lost the first time I entered the facility. I didn't follow the directions the security guard told me about, then I got off on the wrong floor. My mind was everywhere but nowhere.

I felt time was of the essence and there was no room for comprehensive errors. My Mother had no time for my stupidity, so I took some deep breaths and I quickly readjusted my inner GPS and found her room quickly.

We we're just coming off the worst Christmas Eve, Christmas, and New Years, I ever had.

Usually, Christmas Eve is a wonderful time. Her granddaughter who's named after her was born on Christmas Eve. Her name is Ashley Patricia Brown.

This time was spent gift wrapping, drinking eggnog, listening to Nat King Cole and The Motown Christmas album and Mariah Carey. But this year, we didn't feel like spinning any Christmas tunes let alone put up a Christmas tree.

Christmas was not the same in the year of 2021. There was no Christmas dinner. No merry nothing. We just shared worries between my wife and I, and the rest of the family.

I remembered she used to put on her Christmas hat and sing the carols of her favorite recording artists.

She loved decorating and giving out Christmas cards. She looked like one of Santa's cutest helpers. She bathed in the holiday spirit, her joy, and now pain.

We expected to ring in the New Year together as always. I spent over 40 years ringing in the New Year with Mommy, sharing that moment of recollection for all the traveling mercies for the 365 odd days. The goodness God had provided for us and those outside of our immediate circle throughout this and the previous New Year. We thanked Him, and we thanked you.

The timing couldn't be more imperfect, but God is good all the time. Unfortunately, we weren't awarded this New Year's together. We have never spent a holiday without one another.

She was dying from ovarian cancer. It had gone undetected for some time. When she was finally diagnosed, it was at stage four. She could only manage life with it. The word they used was "terminal."

There were procedures done to prevent the spreading and to prolong her life. She also had cocktails that were made up of Benadryl, Steroids, including the various levels of chemotherapy she received weekly. This occurred one year after diagnosis.

I Don't Know Why She Was Proud Of Me

Sometimes she would be too weak to have the drugs administered to her and the doctor would tell her she could take a week off from the medicines and chemo.

When she wasn't on chemo, she would be feeling great and then two days or the next day, she'd feel badly. We were at the point where she had been hospitalized and made comfortable for three weeks.

While she was strong, she made sure her financial obligations were settled. Whatever needed to be taken care of when she became unable to handle her business, it would be handled later.

We were well within the last two weeks of her life. At the Hospice. I did see her getting smaller. There was one time, she became greatly overheated. She was strong enough to take her gown off while my wife assisted her. I grabbed the fan and brought it closer. I think she was having a hot flash. I asked the nurses to come in and check on her. They readjusted her bedding and brought in some fresh ice chips.

During this time, I contacted her friends by text as if she was speaking, letting them know how special they were to her and to smile at the times they shared with one another.

If she mustered up what little strength she had to communicate in whatever form, I allowed it. This was rare, as the precious moments passed, she'd gotten weaker.

I Don't Know Why She Was Proud Of Me

Looking at the sunrays hitting her skin while walking around the bed gazing at her from different angles in different natural sunlight and the pleasantly lit room lights, made me enjoy the moment I had with her. I'd close the door to eliminate the sound that may occur during business hours at the hospice.

This was the last time you would be able to see her breathing. This was the last time you could feel an active pulse. This was the last time to view her eye movement whether under her eye lids or when they'd open. I paid attention to every little detail while she was alive just as I did when I was a little boy admiring and looking up to her.

I often thought of those who love her. Could there have been anything they could've done to help her live. I was given advice on having her eat edibles, to enhance her appetite, or different herbs to put in her food to battle the cancer.

I appreciated all the advice and experiences you've shared with us, but we are now and still at the *till we meet again* phase of her life. Her vital signs we're getting weaker.

Till we meet again means there will be a point when good spirits will reunite based on unselfish deeds and genuine kindness.

I was with Mommy. God was constructing her wings. I was in good hands and so was she. The pain would come to an end.

I Don't Know Why
She Was Proud Of Me

Unimaginable, I would've never thought to be present at this moment. This was in real time. When my Mother used to tell me, her mom died. I took notice to that part of her emotions and her loss.

In memory of my late Grandmother Althea. My Mother is *gonna* be at the *till we meet again* party with her mother.

Thinking back when my wife and I became her healthcare providers. I was happy that we had the means to assist her with transportation, coaching, and binge-watching shows on the internet.

My wife would do her laundry and provide the good daughter approach, above and beyond to everything especially with Mom.

We had to make sure she took her pills at certain times, which my Mother didn't have a problem doing at all by herself.

She had a pill tray and knew all the various bottles and elixirs she had to ingest.

One day she could hardly grasp her walker because she was so weak, so the paramedics carried her by chair lift throughout the second floor, then down the flights of stairs to the foyer. She never returned once the paramedics took her from our home this time.

I swear we were committed to fighting this thing just to have a better quality of life for her. We didn't know we only had a year left.

I Don't Know Why
She Was Proud Of Me

Her vessel had malfunctioned badly. It was preventing her from eating.

One of the procedures we agreed upon was for her not to live with a colostomy bag. She didn't want to have to change and attach that bag, and she didn't want to ask us to assist her with it.

So, when she had the full hysterectomy, which was to better her quality of life, I can recall her saying she doesn't have any use for those parts anymore.

She healed quickly from that, as I watched her wobble throughout the house. She'd pass by the open kitchen area smiling at me. I'd be preparing her some toast or creating a smoothie with cinnamon apple sauce. She loved that.

The doctor said one time she could walk around the block and attempt to do exercises using resistance bands and leg lifts in a chair. She attempted to do them but was not consistent.

I could watch her for days at a time at home looking up at the sky. Watching the birds and planes soar through the air taking in the view of nature that surrounds us.

Since she didn't have any strength to walk around the neighborhood, or get up and down the stairs, she could get some fresh air by sitting on the deck with me. Although a lot of words weren't spoken, I could sense how she felt.

I looked at her in tune with the open cloudless sky. The Orioles, bees, and trees this were good. Sometimes when the sun glared on our deck. I would raise our umbrella. She enjoyed the moment as the cancer was growing inside of her. They eventually gave her chemo pills, and she didn't have to come to the doctor's office weekly anymore, since she was diagnosed a year ago.

We've had many adventures, and precious moments; between my wife, myself, God, and Mommy. If we knew this would be the last year of her life, we could have spent better-quality time with her.

Her eyes clearly said to me, today I'm leaving this earth son. Come to me. She has a tone when she speaks to me where she's serious and not playing. She also has this stare that Mother's give their children without speaking. You can read a Mother's eyes.

Looking at my Mom's expression was as if she was having a spell of pain while trying to communicate with me. I knew I had to pack up and go.

I left my job at 5:00 pm, abruptly. This journey I was about to embark on had me ahead of myself, and the car couldn't get me there fast enough. The time it took me to walk and get in my vehicle, crossing the eight-way intersection, and paying attention to traffic lights, I could've gotten hit by a truck. I used my New York way of thinking and jaywalked through all of the traffic.

I arrived at hospice at 5:45pm. It was getting dark, and it was rainy. I was blessed with safe passage again. I thought to myself it's been me and Mommy since I was a little boy.

I Don't Know Why
She Was Proud Of Me

I'm a grown man about to be fifty and according to the doctors and her stage of cancer this is the end. I knew God has the last say, and I hold on to that while facing the strong possibility that Mom would never sing and dance with me again, or even get up from the bed she is lying in.

I held her hand as she continued to breathe short and slowly. I knew that my touch was the only one that held a bonding DNA of mother and son. I could feel the energy between us and soaked up the seconds she was alive with me.

At this point, it was just her and I and no assistance from an oxygen mask or machines. This was our time our one-on-one. I never looked at her with such admiration and gratitude like this before for all she's done for us.

I know it was a job well done and she should feel accomplished, but I knew deep down inside she wasn't ready to leave us forever and that's why I was still awaiting a miracle.

We were nearing the stages of transitioning.... It was 6:00 pm. Time did not feel like it was going fast or slow. It felt peaceful, welcoming, and lonely. I am an only child, but I felt alone, like when I was younger and didn't quite get it. Why didn't I have any siblings?

I could've used some help bearing this hurt and grief. I was headed towards a brick wall and whatever was in back of me was closing in. I couldn't control this agony it was *gonna* happen whether I had control or not.

I Don't Know Why
She Was Proud Of Me

She had raised her son into a grown man, and she was the most excellent grandmother. What else could she do?

She was a great employee. A good friend to those who accepted and was blessed to have a friendship with her. A good patient. And most of all, she was a child of God. At the pure age of seventy, she convinced me the fight was over and she needed to rest.

I whispered in her ear, "Now you can rest Mommy. I'm here."

She has scriptures on her wall, not many, but her daily prayers and some words of encouragement. This was during a time I reflect upon before her diagnosis. She was a cheerful giver who didn't expect much in return. She was a beautiful soul. Even in business, I was proud of her. I sat with her as a witness that she had done well by God.

I assured her she is God's daughter, and she has a son and he's *gonna* help and be courteous to folks as she intended me to do.

I also whispered she'd earned her wings and had received forgiveness. I mentioned that she would never have to worry anymore and that she would be smiling from heaven. We will be alright and that I love her.

I continued to hold her hand which seemed like it was getting stiff, and her breathing was getting slower and harder. She was starting to transition.

I held my phone to her ear, and I played her favorite songs. Songs that I've seen and heard her play on her own time with the passion and delivery the singer intended it to have.

Songs that I've seen her dance to and become one with word for word in happiness, joy, and conflict like when she sang Barbara Streisand and Barry Gibb's 1980 hit "Guilty." She felt the music and celebrated the band's works as they intended it to be enjoyed. My Mother would sing her heart out at times.

I could envision her having a good ole time with her wings on in heaven. Spinning around to the music of Lisa Stansfield singing "Been Around the World" smiling looking youthful and rejuvenated.

I selected songs from a playlist I made in her honor, featuring Patti Labelle and Gladys Knight. These were touching songs that spoke of togetherness with family and friends. I really felt her compassion and rhythmic expressions when she played the album by Marvin Gaye "What's Going On."

During a time when Black Pride was at its height and artist spoke from that perspective of love and unity for one another.

This country's government didn't want this music, and culture, and art, but it made a profit for them as they copied the talent. They would invest minimally, and the return would be generational wealth leaving the Black artist penniless amidst his or her career or even put in jail.

I Don't Know Why
She Was Proud Of Me

These soulful times and songs touched my Mother's heart and soul. It transferred to me in her womb before she gave birth to me. She got emotional and tearful and joyful listening to this music.

I tried to create a soundtrack for her returning to her father in heaven. I played songs by Luther Vandross. He was one of her favorite balladeers.

She had gotten incredibly angry at me one time because I misplaced a DVD of his live concert. She threatened me if I didn't find it.

My wife laughed as I searched for the DVD awfully hard, as if she were my little sister watching her big brother getting in trouble.

I tore the house up so I can find it. Eventually, she calmed down once it was found and she got into her groove, snapping her fingers, moving her body, and singing along.

I saw her singing his song "Creep" in her own way.

My Mother didn't have the pipes like Gladys or Patti, but this Patty which they called her for short, did her thing. She would've been a good karaoke singer.

She understood people and could tell good ones from bad ones. She had some bad experiences with bad people that mostly came from men, but overall, she was a small lady with a big heart full of love, and that's how some men may have taken advantage of her womanhood.

I Don't Know Why
She Was Proud Of Me

But you could count on my Mother if you needed something, that's coming from me as I held the phone steady so that she could enjoy the music and songs she loved one last time with me.

I could hear her singing Whitney Houston and CeCe Winans' song from the Waiting to Exhale soundtrack "Count on Me." *She would really go in on that song,* I thought to myself while "That's What Friends Are For" by Dionne Warwick and Friends played from the playlist.

"Friendship Train" by Gladys Knight and the Pips played. This song reminded me of good people enjoying themselves for the sake of all humanity, throughout the United States of America.

My intentions were for my Mother to hear this music and remind her that she's enroute to where good people exist.

The horrors and complications that she'd witnessed and lived through here on God's planet, would not be allowed to infect friendships that were created to last a lifetime and beyond in heaven.

My Mother was a friend of God riding the friendship train. She was ready to shake his hand and journey with him wherever her stop may be.

My Mommy was a peaceful woman. She was trustworthy and loyal. Her friends would know her for being engaging, humorous, and a joy to be around.

I Don't Know Why
She Was Proud Of Me

She was witty and smart, but she never got a driver's license, though. One thing for sure, she would never be anyone's driver.

She once told me her brother once tried to teach her how to drive, and she put the car in reverse and caused a bad accident. Ever since then she never attempted learning to drive again.

She stayed in her lane as a good passenger. I continued remembering many precious moments we shared, as I held the phone gently to her ear.

You are my friend, by Patti Labelle played as her breathing continued to get heavier.

I sat by her bedside looking into her eyes and feeling stuck in a place of melody and memories, and the uncertainty that I would no longer be able to see her smile again.

I was still seeking and looking for this miracle. While coming to terms with her dying, I battled with the harsh reality while preparing my heart for its breaking. "Anyone who had a Heart" played by Luther Vandross."

It was now 7:30 pm. The sun had dimmed to nightfall and the moon lit the sky. The room we were in was slightly lit too, just the light from the television which showed waterfalls and calming forest visuals. I had been there for almost three hours.

I learned that where I was and what I was doing has not been done before. I was being blessed with the opportunity to be with her while she transitions. I made it on time. I was available, and I was thankful for traveling mercies once more.

My last two selections of songs were from Marsha Ambrosius and Anthony Hamilton. I chose them because of their chemistry together and vocally there unmatched.

I may have heard this song before while I was looking for songs on the internet. This combination was suitable for this time of the day. They sang a rendition of Stevie Wonder's Song "As." This version is beautiful. This is the message I wanted to leave with my Mother in a beautifully harmony of a man and a woman.

I wanted her to remember this melody. I wanted her to relax now because she had done her fighting on planet earth. She lived through various rounds of strong chemo. She was blessed and I felt the time was nearing. I was being strong and supportive.

I wanted her to know. I would love her until the sky vanishes and all the stars in space twinkle just for her, for the next 15 minutes. I played the original version of the song. This is the version of the song I was introduced to.

My Uncle and my Mother used to play it all the time. They sang and grooved to it all night long on replay. I felt the vibe that it provided as a child.

I thought it was a masterpiece at a young age. I listened to the instrumentation of Stevie Wonder playing all the instruments and singing background harmony.

I Don't Know Why
She Was Proud Of Me

I watched Mother and my Uncle at times become air musicians, acting out as if they were playing the instruments.

I looked over at her as I always did. She was still. Her face was frozen with her mouth open. Her eyes were glossy and wide open. Her gown showed no movement, looking at her chest to see if she was breathing. I checked her pulse, I felt her hand, I got up and looked at my Mother, I ran and alerted the nurses.

They checked her pulse. this was their profession, They set the mood. They've witnessed another loved one leave this facility.

This was my harsh reality. They told me she has transitioned.

At 7:45 P.M. my Mother took her last breath. I collapsed and the tears from my body just released.

I released an involuntary scream and cried out. One of the nurses had to console me, while the other nurse tended to her empty vessel.

They called my wife and informed her of what happened. They felt I may need assistance driving, because I was not in any decent shape to drive at that moment. I gathered myself and stood in front of her bed. I spoke with her and said Mommy you're not suffering anymore, but selfishly I thought what about me? I felt a part of me was missing. I felt half man half broken.

I Don't Know Why
She Was proud Of Me

My wife arrived shortly thereafter and went hysterical. She cried her eyes out and stood at the foot of the bed, while viewing her body. She mentioned that mother could now rest in peace and not be in pain any longer.

The nurses made it known that funeral arrangements and removal of the body needed to be done in a timely manner. I understood, it was time to move forward with the funeral and viewing arrangements. I called my cousin and told her that her Auntie had left us. She cried and asked if there was anything she could do. I told her I would update her as soon as we figured out what we were going to do next.

I called her six Grandchildren: Alysha, Lisa, Magnifisense, Shakeem, Jeremiah, and Zachariah. I let them know that Grandma has gone to heaven, and she will always love them.

We had no arrangements made; and it was getting late. Her body had to be removed by midnight.

My wife Eudy called Auntie Cheryl, and she helped us over the phone to find a funeral home. This began a new chapter in my life. My life was altered and a part of me ended too. I remember when my Mother was alive, and she introduced me as her son to her friends' colleagues or whomever.

I would never hear her introduce me as her son again. We were at the *till we meet again* stage in our lives, me at age forty-nine, and she was seventy. I wouldn't have that joy of seeing her in real time going out eating, partying, and enjoying life.

As a child she used to say, "Billy you get on my last nerves." I think I got on her last nerves just to hear her say that, over and over again. I think I enjoyed her chastising me. I was obedient most of the time, but her rage entertained me. As her only child looking back it was her that was my friend.

I could remember even the small things throughout the day she taught and raised me by, and now I say good morning to her urn, and I cherish the life we once lived together.

My wife of twelve years had lost her mom and dad when she was in her early teens. She was close to her parents and a daddy's girl.

She wished she could've grown closer with her mom and have had her father walk her down the aisle on our wedding day. Her Uncle stood in for him. She grew remarkably close to my Mother as a daughter would to her mother.

I've never had a loss like this before. This was different for me. I felt lost and dizzy. I asked God to strengthen my heart, emotional state, of course my wife, family, and friends as well.

I decided on having her cremated, because I wanted her next to me and not in the ground outside in the cemetery.

I Don't Know Why
She Was Proud Of Me

She wanted to be cremated as well because she didn't want bugs crawling on her, as she lie lifeless in a casket. My aunt Mimi said the same thing, I will tell you about her later on.

We had the nicest funeral home and the staff there was fabulous. They did a wonderful job with the arrangements, and presentation. The ceremony was streamed online live for those who couldn't make it.

I continued to feel weird. I continued to think moving forward, There will always be something missing from my mornings, afternoons, and evenings. It's my Mother calling me throughout the day on my cell just to talk and saying to me, "Goodnight Billy."

I was unfamiliar with this part of life. I never went a day without her being there for me. I consistently spend time with her urn in her room along with my wife's mother's urn Ms. Tina.

She happened to transition on the 28th of January. My Mother passed on the 20th of January. Their urns are beside the bed where mom once laid every night.

I didn't think I would ever have to make the decision to have her cremated. Let alone have her deleted from the living.

This type of pain is unexplainable, it's one you would have to go through yourself. No one can tell you about how you should feel when you lose your mom, because everyone's journey with their mother is different. Some folks weren't close to their mother like me, and mines were. Some folks never got to know their mothers then there's others whose relationships unfortunately didn't have the time to grow.

I didn't believe what had just happened. This seemed like a nightmare. I wanted to stop dreaming and get on with my real life, the one with Mommy being a cancer survivor.

The one thought that ran through my mind was that it's Saturday and I'm *gonna* make my Mother some grits, eggs, and sausage for breakfast. She would shake her salt, pepper on the grits, and mix it with butter then she would say, "It's yummy."

I believe that I brought the youth out of her, it felt as if the parental roles had changed at times as I think back.

She would ask if we were having movie night and request ice cream. She loved it. After she'd eaten all of hers, she'd eat my wife's vanilla and chocolate chip Haagen-Dazs® ice cream, too. That's my wife's favorite flavor and it became Mommy's.

I was unprepared. No one is prepared for a loss as big as this one. I never listened to my Mom when she told me she wouldn't always be here.

I didn't even listen to the doctors when they told me the cancer was terminal. I just thought I'd be blessed enough with a life being with my Mother happily ever after forever and ever.

I Don't Know Why She Was proud Of Me

I needed therapy. I needed to see what it could do for me; a lot of people told me I should see a therapist. Because they may have been looking on the outside of our relationship and knew how strong it was. Some tried therapy and it helped. I felt like this was my worst blunder. I couldn't help my Mother. I couldn't save her and.... I don't know why she was proud of me....

I am not a wealthy man, nor highly intelligent; nor am I athletic. I never raised my voice towards her, and I never swore at her. I never called her out of her name. I always addressed my Mother as Mommy. I respected her.

It was her that taught me my mannerisms and respect for others, especially the elders. She always told me to put a handle on a person's name, pertaining to Mr. or Mrs.

Hold the door open for a lady ... ladies first, especially if she has little children with her and so on and so forth.

I can recall some pivotal moments; we shared in our forty years together on this planet. While Growing up, I was a knucklehead. When I look back, I'm ashamed of my behavior, towards my community and women. I don't think I embarrassed my Mother that much, or maybe I did.

I know at times she had to vent to her co-workers and her brother. She'd suffer in silence before and in front of me, but it was over now.

She could Rest In Peace (R.I.P.). She survived seventy years on this planet, twenty of them, I had nothing to do with. She was not well traveled. In fact, she did not own a passport. We were working on getting her one. She really did not enjoy flying at all, especially the part where your ears get clogged.

My wife and I once took her and one of our sons on vacation to Disney World in Orlando, Florida. She did not like to be in a closed tight space for long, especially when she'd gotten older.

She definitely didn't appreciate TSA telling her to throw her perfume away because the size of the bottle exceeded their size limitations. She wasn't impatient, she got annoyed, and flying is not for everyone. Her ears didn't unclog for days. At that point, she was through with traveling by plane and that's just what she'd say. "Billy I'm thru *wit* it!"

She was a finicky eater too; she did not like mayonnaise, only in potato salad and macaroni salad. That was it. She preferred mustard on her sandwiches, and when she made sandwiches, they looked so neat, and she always cut them diagonally.

She didn't drink milk or coffee. She didn't like beer either. She liked her Pepsi and Ginger ale.

She was a Harlemite. One of those folks who could live forever on one block in New York City where everything is just steps away. Trouble around every corner and the city never sleeps.

I Don't Know Why
She Was proud Of Me

New Yorkers do not need to own a vehicle to move around, to get to work, or to visit other New Yorkers. The transit system worked just fine, and my Mother utilized it every day going to work, catching the number three train to Chambers Street, or transferring to the number four or five train, ending up at The Brooklyn Bridge stop, and doing the same thing coming back home Mondays through Fridays.

She was content as a young woman, and she took care of me the best way she could. I was born a breached baby, as she told me.... I gave her a hard time during birth, I had a dresser drawer for a bassinet when she first entered motherhood. We were poor.

As I was told, my aunt Mimi used to play the James Brown record "Get on the good foot," and I would start getting on my good foot dancing to the song. My Mother used to say I tickled her when I did that. Later on in life, she continued to make sure I had a roof over my head, and I got upgraded to having my own room. She made sure I had food to eat, and a bed to lay my head to sleep.

My Mother was a young lady. Just figuring it out, being a single mom in a crazy version of New York City. She needed time to become a stronger woman and a mother. She had me when she was twenty and raised me basically by herself.

I was blessed with the opportunity to take care of her in her time of need as she had gotten older.

I Don't Know Why She Was Proud Of Me

I lived to see that everything she couldn't do for me when I was younger or when she was younger, she made up for it when I got older.

When I had kids, she helped me with raising my children. Just being Patty. Just being Grandma. Just being Patricia Laverne Brown.

She used to always tell me that she was glad I was a boy because she didn't know how to braid or do hair, and basically, raising a girl in the 70s would be more difficult than raising a boy, for her.

She loved the way I grasped the masculine perspective of being head strong and a responsible adult. When I sort of matured, she saw me embrace fatherhood at an early age, and she helped the Mothers of my children co-parent with me too.

Surviving my boyhood made an imperfect flawed male. She was incredibly pleased with my upbringing and outcome. She respected me too.

One thing she loved about me was, I stopped being in the streets on those corners, and in those blocks, and she didn't have to see me doing time in jail. We did it well together as Mother and son.

I'm relieved my Mother didn't have to endure the pain of burying me. We know some mothers who we've encountered in our daily walks, which went through that; but we lived on until we weren't granted our union of Mother and son any longer.

I Don't Know Why
She Was Proud Of Me

She was the best she could be. I was right there watching her come home from work. Sometimes we'd meet at the train station, or she'd invite me and the grandkids to her job at One Police Plaza and have lunch.

We'd even do some shopping at the fruit and nuts store, or we'd go to J&R Music world and do some CD and DVD shopping. This store was once in the Financial District area of New York.

A lot of stores and businesses were there but no longer are in business due to the tragic 9/11 attacks on The World Trade Center and also how streaming changed the way we purchase music and movies.

My Mommy was a survivor of that tragedy which was one of the worst days in New York history in America.

On Friday's when she got paid, she would stop at the liquor store, and get her a pint of Bacardi Dark and a pack of Winston's cigarettes. She'd cut on her records on The Big Television Record Player Combo unit and sing for hours. The songs of Stephanie Mills, Earth Wind and Fire, Al Green, Gladys Knight, Luther Vandross, and The Friends of Distinction. She told me that her graduating class sang one of their songs called "This Generation" at her junior high school graduation.

She was a petite woman with long black hair. She always wore cute outfits and nice dresses in the summer. She liked wearing T-shirts too. She didn't wear heels, She always wore flats, and loved to wear baseball caps when she put her hair in a ponytail.

I Don't Know Why
She Was Proud Of Me

Yes. I grew up right before her eyes. From a boy to a man. And in her later years, I was able to create an environment for her to feel comfortable in retirement.

I may not have been able to buy her a house, but she lived with me and my wife. She was able to relax as a carefree retiree and she enjoyed it.

I can recall one morning she was just lying down getting ready to watch her shows for the day. This was her regular routine. I was getting ready for work. I knocked on her door and I greeted her. This was our daily routine. I said, "Good morning, Mommy" like I always did. She replied, "Good morning, Billy." In her feminine lovable voice. I smiled.

She always calls me Billy, but when she's angry I mean REAL! Angry, she calls me WILLIAM. I haven't heard my name in that tone of voice in a long time.

As the morning progressed, I saw an invitation on the news to be a member of a Senior Citizen Program up the road from where we lived. I copied the number down and gave it to her. That morning she called it and ever since then, her life went in a grand direction. She was accepted in the senior center at a new renovated location. She was able to meet people who didn't have concept of the gritty streets of New York where we'd come from.

She loved getting up in the morning, getting into prayer; getting herself together, then calling the transportation company to take her back and forth to the center.

I Don't Know Why
She Was Proud Of Me

But every county has its ups and downs. My Mother, and my wife traveled from Maryland then to Queens New York, to see her doctors and her dentist because the state of Maryland wouldn't take her medical coverage.

We celebrated the holidays, birthdays, and sang the Happy Birthday song the normal way, then we'd remix it and sing it The Stevie Wonder way.

We also celebrated the births of new babies born. She loved her niece and nephew, her great nieces, and nephews too. She was one of the fortunate ones who attended her grandkids' graduations. And spent several monumental moments with family, friends and the extended family, and her new friends she met at the senior center.

She really got into party mode on the 4th of July. Folks would have cookouts, play music, cards, etc. Then when nightfall hit, there would be a local fireworks display. She also loved watching the Thanksgiving Day Parade on television. That was a signal that the Christmas Season has started. She'd enjoy watching the Macy's fireworks spectacular on 34th street too. We actually went there once, and we had an enjoyable time.

She maintained friendships, and stayed connected with colleagues, that she bonded with during her career with the NYPD. She was a contributor to society and joined a church in Maryland. She tithed, prayed, paid taxes, and believed in Jesus. We prayed to him often together; especially when she got the diagnosis about having stage four ovarian cancer.

She was a lady that took care of herself, she enjoyed playing Nintendo, bowling, and watching Law and Order. She loved watching game shows too. Let's Make a Deal, The Price is Right, and of course The Family Feud, with the host Richard Dawson, from back in the day, and now with the comedy Steve Harvey.

She created a household where you'd come in the front door, and you could smell dinner cooking. It would be cold outside, but warm and cozy in her apartment.

I did my chores as a kid. I assisted her by sweeping, mopping, dusting, and cleaning the bathroom, hallway, and living room.

She'd take care of the kitchen, but somehow, we still had roaches, flies, and mice, and we had those nasty looking fly traps that hung from the ceiling.

She used to always get on me about washing the dishes. She'd say, "It's only me and you in the house. Why is there dishes in the sink?" I finally understood her frustrations, so I started washing the dishes. When I did that, she was calm, and her stress levels went down.

But she was probably seeing grey hair growing from her scalp back then from the bull crap I put her through as a kid. I don't know why she was proud of me.

We had to wash our clothes by hand using a box of Trend Detergent, and wring them out, then hang them on

I Don't Know Why She Was proud Of Me

the window sill to dry; or place them on the steam, then hang some out the window on a clothesline with clothesline pins attached to them so they wouldn't fall in the basement.

I am the only son of Patricia and William Brown. Both of my Grandfathers were named William Brown.

My Mother and Father were never married. They lived on 147th Street in Harlem in the same block. We're all from the tenement buildings in Harlem.

One time she made chitterlings; they were good. And they stunk the whole apartment up. She must've gotten the recipe from my grandmother or her mother. She got the ones in the white container. I tried them, I can't front, some people know how to hook them joints up with rice, green peppers, celery, onions, and seasonings. Occasionally, with some bird's eye frozen spinach from the box.

My Mother was gifted with cooking talent and could put together a mean pastrami on rye sandwich. She also made a delicious chili too, steak, potatoes, pot roast, baked macaroni and cheese, spaghetti with meat sauce and 145th street rice, etc. Many people who were blessed to taste her cooking were pleased with the meals she prepared.

One thing I learned from living with a woman is always knock on the door before entering because when you're the only child, a son, and you hear noises behind a door when your Mom has company; Ya might want to knock before barging in; checking to see what's going on. I'm just saying.

She taught me to always knock before entering a door; and always show kindness to everyone.

I don't think my mom thought I'd make it through my childhood. I was very troublesome. I became a whole different man, once I grew into adulthood, and fatherhood.

I even got a Letter of Good behavior, from the Chief of Patrol Office in New York.

I was taught by organizations in the inner city such as the C V C (City Volunteer Corps.), S Y E P (Summer Youth Employment Program.) and of course Street Wise Partners in Harlem NYC.

I learned how to navigate through the corporate world, from the mailroom level. They taught me to play the game or be the game. What that basically means is act professionally and speak correct English. Be welcoming and be courteous, be a team player, and when your shift is over and business is completed, then you can truly be yourself.

Later on in life, I learned that Corporate America's private sector has a lot of racism embedded into it. It's not what you know; it's who you know, and who likes you. It's hard to get a promotion when you're Black, and people will stab you in the back, some people lie to get to the top or to save their jobs.

I Don't Know Why
She Was proud Of Me

There's thievery from the executive offices down to the mailroom, and companies will use you to their advantage.

My Mother saw me engaging with these folks. Using street smarts and social skills to survive within Corporate America, particularly the private sector. She appreciated my efforts on being a role model and positive influence on my children. I've come a long way since my teens, and early twenties. She knew my babies needed their daddy....

In her younger years, she was quite popular, and she hung with her best friend Marlene. They grew up together with a whole array of friends from Harlem. I wasn't there, but what I found out was she was the youngest of two brothers. Gerald and Leslie. Leslie the oldest who was killed in Harlem.

He was the first person I saw with a golden can that he drank out of. He drank Olde English 800 malt liquor and to me it looked shiny and exciting, sometimes it was in a paper bag. I would take it out the bag and taste it. Later on in life, I drank 40 ounce bottles of beer when I got older. This was a bigger golden giant bottle, compared to what he was drinking.

He was a street cat, and he was a ladies' man. He also was a heroin addict who stole from others. I heard in conversations he was a thief from some of the elders, my Great Auntie, and his girlfriend. I heard people did not trust my Uncle Leslie. He had stolen before. He also hung around drug addicts, and they roamed the streets of Harlem and did their thing.

One day under his watch, I was attempting to play basketball in between 147th Street and 7th and 8th Avenue. I jumped up trying to dunk the ball, but I fell and cut my hand very deep. I needed stitches. My Mother was furious at him, but in all actuality, I was a scrub. I could not play basketball. I didn't inherit that talent from my Dad. He was gifted.

I also heard a story about Uncle Les, that he died because he couldn't take heroin withdrawal once he had been hospitalized and his dumb ass friends came and gave him a hotshot and he died in the hospital. Poor Uncle Les.

There is a movie entitled "The Brother from Another Planet." It's rare, but this movie could give you a realization and visualization of the block in The Village of Harlem in the 70s and 80s and even up to the 90s would put fear in the average person because of its spooky, but dangerous appearance in the daytime and especially at night.

The burnt out abandoned buildings had windows that were either boarded up with wood or busted out from within them. Dusty bent mailboxes with their doors off. Graffiti tags were thrown up all over them. Some apartment doors were closed, and some were broken into.

The center block sealed entrances of the buildings were broken through. Wino's, dope fiends, squatters, dealers, and soon to be crackheads, would find shelter and

I Don't Know Why She Was proud Of Me

comfort within these abandoned properties. Not only were there abandoned buildings, but there were abandoned schools too. These images will permanently be stained in my mind as I actually entered them and wandered around one of the uninhabited dead school.

I saw the abandoned library with its open area dusty chairs and no books on the dusty shelves the Dewey decimal systems were removed. I explored deeper to where the pool was where students once swam as an extracurricular activity, but the spookiest of them all was the abandoned auditorium because it's a large open space with rows of unoccupied ragged seats leading to the immense darkened creepy stage. I was frightened but I loved to explore since I was a baby boy. I didn't want to get lost in there forever, so I was being cautious on how far I went into this worn down neglected inactive school.

My Uncle Gerald lived to see his grandchildren. He became happily married, and had two of his own kids, a girl named Kanika and a boy named Gerald, his junior. My Uncle Gerald was a wise man, tech savvy and was a mathematician. I used to look thru his archives of thick scientific books, tools, and his papers he had laying around, now that I look back. He may have been studying to obtain another degree.

He drove cabs for a living when he was younger and attended city college in upper Manhattan where he met his future wife to be my Auntie Serena. He was a smoker too. His favorite choice of cigarette was True Blue. I didn't know how dangerous smoking was back then, as I

I Don't Know Why
She Was Proud Of Me

watched him drive with me in the passenger seat, at times I glanced at the box where the cigarettes were stored and even the box looked scientific with its logo and blue silver lettering.

He loved people and the social climate of Blacks in America affected him deeply. He was my soul brother number one. He was a chess player, a spades player, and he even taught me how to play parcheesi. I learned a lot from watching him.

I learned how to make lasagna, I learned how to coordinate your feet in a car while driving and steering and most of all how to be smooth. He was a favorite to all the aunties and a legend to me.

She was a Harlem girl born in the early 50s. She would tell me when I was vandalizing the city, as a youth. She would say, "Billy, you'll be gone, but those street corner's will still be here."

She had a feminine approach with tough love. She loved me. She cared for me … and when I was a baby, she'd hand wash my diapers, because I was allergic to pampers, as an infant.

She loved music from the 70's, all the way up to Silk Sonic in 2022. She wished Bruno Mars was her boyfriend…. But I think she wanted to grow old with Teddy Pendergrass. She liked rough looking masculine men.

I Don't Know Why
She Was proud Of Me

I was raised in an OFF THE HOOK HABITAT. Meaning that there was crazy stuff going on all the time around me. She disciplined me all the way until I became 16 years of age. This is when I got out of control, and she needed my Father to help. He was always around the corner, or on the corner. When I became of age, I tracked him down, on the corner, or around the corner, or at his other stash apartments. If it weren't for his escapades, I wouldn't have discovered and fell in love with HipHop music. My Dad had finished his jail bid and I'd catch him on the corner sometimes. He'd given me a few bucks here and there.

I love my stepsisters Melinda and Nefertiti. We all have different takes on our Dad by the way he treated our mothers and his children. My Sisters mean the world to me. I was the only son. As I watched them interact with their other siblings, I envied them sometimes because when I went home to my house, I had no one to play with or talk to. Like maternal brothers and sisters do, at times I felt like a step child, and I was.

She was in love with my Father, but he didn't love her the same. She wanted to be his wife, but he married another woman named Linda. She was a nice lady. May God rest her soul.

They called my Father "Billy Lip" in the streets. He was in and out of jail while Mommy struggled with raising me on her own. Legend also says, he was good at playing basketball. I never witnessed this myself.

I Don't Know Why She Was Proud Of Me

I wore Alexanders and Conway shit in the winter, with a nappy Skully hat.

We'd frequent the welfare center, as mother and child. I think I can recall a social worker coming by making sure a man doesn't stay with us. She would be annoyed at the questions she had to answer on this stretched out form a couple of times a year. I felt frustrated and bored every time we went there. Sometimes we stayed there all day waiting to see her caseworker. I think they would even tell her to come back another day because they had to close for the day.

I could smell the franks boiling, with the hot sausages, relish, and cooked onions at the stand, which stood on the corner. We hardly ever stopped at the Frank Stand to get anything. When we did, they were delicious, especially with a canned soda. People called them dirty dogs.

I didn't have any friends during my early phases of boyhood. I stayed with Mommy majority of the time. I was exposed to her world, a world of laughter, peculiar characters, Gloria... and Herman. Herman had a club foot and drove a white four-by-four.... There was also Sam Trina..., Jo-Ann, and Alonzo.

Jo-Ann had a brother named Leonard aka The Space Ghost. He was the best car washer in Harlem on 145th Street.

You'd see Alpo, Rich Porter, and Azie whizzing by on dirt bikes, motorcycles or gliding by in exotic foreign cars in all colors. They were his clientele - The Harlemites....

I Don't Know Why She Was proud Of Me

King Sun The Legendary Rapper dropped jewels to me from time to time as he passing through.

As I mentioned, her buddies were folks who enjoyed drinking beer, and rum, laughing and joking, and some even enjoyed sniffing a lil cocaine.

The sweet smell of Cheeba also loomed around the stoop which wasn't her thing, but she'd take a puff one or two sometimes.

I was watching her. As I said before, her thing was the rum and cigarettes. This was a smell later on in life I became quite familiar with.

All on one stoop in front of the building, she never sniffed or injected anything…. The women and men I was exposed to left an impression on me. Some good and some bad.

The women raised their children and provided stability and comfort for their families while the men would play their position in the streets. Some hustled, some were retirees, and some were straight alcoholics, and some got infected by the nearing crack wave too. Some survived and thrived as we speak today … and some died from various health complications.

As the only child, I often became curious and nosey listening through walls to hear my mother's conversations. Rummaging through her dresser drawers, going through her pocketbooks and stuff. I can reflect on my childhood very clearly.

I Don't Know Why She Was Proud Of Me

My Mother was nurturing. I don't know why she was proud of me. I'll always love her dearly. Every now and then she'd prepare breakfast eggs, grits, and bacon. Sometimes it was grits and sardines with the red sauce. That was delicious. Other times she would serve it with toast and Parkay® butter. Although I was a boy possibly seven or eight years old, she never bought me any Cap'n Crunch®, Apple Jacks® a preteen, he lived in the Bronx, nor Froot Loops® cereal. And if she didn't make breakfast, I didn't eat except in the summertime, I'd get the free breakfast and lunch from the government programs they had in schools.

For dinner she prepared lima beans with smoked turkey necks, rice, and corn. The kids would tease me about that the next day when we'd discuss what we had for dinner. She also made liver, mashed potatoes with gravy, green peppers onions, and spinach.

I loved her potato salad and baked macaroni and cheese. Occasionally, she'd make Jell-O®, with fruit cocktail mixed in it. She also made baked ribs with white rice and buttered seasoned corn. The ribs were the kind where the bone would melt in your mouth, with the barbecue sauce. They were juicy and when you chew the bone, you'd taste all the seasonings. Her baked chicken hit like that too. I used to eat the bone marrow it was so Good.

Occasionally she'd make a yellow cake with chocolate frosting. She would always let me lick the bowl and the spoon afterwards. Mmmmm!

I Don't Know Why She Was proud Of Me

Later on in life she would tell her grandkids that she cooked with love. I didn't have any experience on how to operate the stove or cook. That's untill My Great Aunt Muriel aka Aunt Mimi moved in. She was my Mother's aunt, my grandfather's sister. They are survived by their Sister Samia. We called her Aunt Mimi, but her name was Muriel Brown.

She was a short woman who was tough! She told me how she carried a 22-caliber pistol in her boot, when she was a teenager.

She always said save $5.00 out of everything you make, and she kept packs of cigarettes in the freezer. She loved smoking Chesterfield King cigarettes. I come from a family of smokers, and her favorite cigarette was Winston.

My Aunt once told a doctor she would stop smoking when she died. She also told me Browns don't come in ugly…. We are The Browns, and my aunt was conceded. No joke.

My Mother loved my great aunt like a daughter loves her mother. Since my Grandmother had died, she probably was the one she gravitated to the most for female guidance. She lived with us for a while, and she took over my room.

She once punched me in my face because I talked back to her, then she turned on the television and watched her favorite baseball teams play, the Los Angeles Dodgers or the Atlanta Braves.

I Don't Know Why
She Was Proud Of Me

I told my Mother what she did to me, and she spoke to my Aunt Mimi about it, she shut her down too. She felt Aunt Mimi's iron fist and disciplinarian approach. Just because she was grown, Aunt Mimi still demanded respect as the elder. My Mother *kinda* wished she hadn't let Aunt Mimi stay with us because she was still young and wanted to have fun, but she had a son, and Aunt Mimi was from the old school, and she wasn't having it.

She was on *some* your child comes first before any of that hanging out mess. And I *ain't* no babysitter either, she would state. At this stage, it kind of felt like she and I were siblings, and Aunt Mimi was our mother, but my mother was grown, and she did what she wanted anyway.

Aunt Mimi was a bully but a strong Black woman who was seasoned by the streets, and hardships that all women, not just Black ones faced throughout the 50's and 60's. She drove a school bus too; her legacy would span over the Browns for two more generations.

Aunt Mimi despised Mother's boyfriend Warren. She was aware of the physical and mental abuse he was dishing out to her. She did not want to be around him.

One Saturday morning, I got up and sat in the kitchen while Mom was asleep, and my Aunt Mimi was up. She asked me what are you doing sitting here.

I said, "I'm waiting for Mommy to cook breakfast...."

She said, "If you wait for someone to cook for you, you'll probably never eat."

I Don't Know Why
She Was proud Of Me

She then said, "Let me teach you how to cook."

She said the first thing you do is, "Wash your hands and make sure your cooking area is neat and clean; as you cook, clean your bowls, knives, cooking utensils, etc.; that way you don't have dishes piling up in the sink, and you don't have a lot of work to do after you finish."

"Now, the first thing is scrambled eggs."

She taught me flame control, and how to clean up after myself after I cook.

I became a natural at cooking. I mastered the basics. I started making my Mommy breakfast in bed. I could tell Aunt Mimi was impressed, because she'd be walking by the kitchen inspecting and checking on me while smiling as if to say, "Good job Billy."

I made her a plate too. It wasn't long before she moved to Rochester, New York to help her daughter Barbara.

From what I can recall and by using my ear hustling abilities, they didn't have a great relationship. She favored my Mother over Barbara, her natural daughter, and she loved my Uncle Gerald. She called him Prayers.

I love cooking, and I loved fire. One day I can recall my cousin Kanika and I were in the kitchen playing. I got ahold of some matches and burned a piece of paper towel. I had no idea how fast it burns, so I tried to put it out. I threw it in the garbage. It lit the entire bag of garbage on fire and burned one of my Mother's chairs. She was enraged and my cousin Kanika was like my Robin, and I was Batman.

Kanika was amazed at the blaze. Mother and Uncle Gerald smelled smoke. "WILLIAM!" My Mother shouted while they were in the living room listening to the Shaft album, by Isaac Hayes. They rushed into the Kitchen and quickly extinguished the fire on the chair that the garbage sat on.

My Mother was upset at me. She cut the stove on and placed my hand on one of the eyes on the stove just enough for me to feel the heat but not long enough to cause severe burns to my skin. I was traumatized. I believe Kanika may have ran. From that day on, I realized that you have to be responsible with fire. It can burn your whole house down, and it can get you in deep trouble.

My maternal Grandfather, William Brown, was a cool dude as I can remember. He had a nice apartment in the upper Bronx. I remember he used to always have a joint in his mouth, and he'd be playing albums by Maze featuring Frankie Beverly and Quincy Jones.

I remember times when Mother, uncle, aunt, and my cousin would gather at Grandpa's house on Christmas. His house was somewhere located on 224th and 225th Streets, by the number two train in the Bronx. He had remarried after divorcing my paternal Grandmother.

This devastated her and her brothers. She slightly resented my Step Grandmother, respectfully, and I don't think Aunt Mimi was feeling her that much either.

I Don't Know Why
She Was proud Of Me

She had two daughters of her own, and one of them had two boys. I never got really close to them, but we're family still and that was the only Grandmother I've known.

My Mother was a member of a broken family, and I felt her pain. My Paternal Grandmother had died when I was just a toddler, I never got to know her, but I think my Grandfather was unfaithful to her, and it really affected his children possibly to the point where alcohol and heroin was used to soothe the emotional pains especially felt by the eldest sibling Leslie.

My Mother and I once lived in an apartment in the Bronx on Aqueduct Avenue across the street from Bronx Community College. I was now old enough to go outside and play by myself with little to know supervision.

I had no friends, so I'd play in the dirt with ants, or I'd find friendship in other insects, such as roaches. I'd take them apart and remove their heads, legs and eggs and watch them react to the dismantling. I'd catch mice and place them in Christmas stockings, then go to school. I couldn't wait to get home, so that I could play with them. I was extremely disappointed when I came home and found out it didn't survive. That's when I learned living things need oxygen to breathe.

I'd explore the insides of abandoned apartments within the neighborhood. She always told me to be in the house when it gets dark or at eight o'clock. I hadn't mastered reading a clock yet, so I tried my best to be in when it got dark. My Mother was strict.

One day, I was wandering around the neighborhood. I would do this often because I was an adventurous child. I went to the library on the side of this high-rise building, and guess who I bumped into as I was turning the corner? My Father and his new family.

My Father and I would cross paths often in the street. I figured this out as I got older. He had my stepsister Melinda and she had two siblings Mushie and Richie. I never knew their real names. But we became close, and they alongside their mom Evelyn welcomed me into their home.

They had a nice apartment, with an elevator within the building. I can recall that nice building smell kind of like fresh oil on machinery with a hint of lemon.

As a child, when I'd visited, I felt a sense of welcome without a place to stay. I'd see my Father and Evelyn laid up chillin' in the bedroom.

Her kids were in their early teens, in the living room with plush carpet, nice big color television and overall spacious luxurious living. I had no knowledge of real estate, but I would later learn this was a condo. My Mom and I lived down the block in a nice building.

I love my Dad. I love my sisters and their siblings. They called me Lil Billy, and my Father was Big Billy. He was a dark-skinned man from Harlem. He was rumored

I Don't Know Why
She Was proud Of Me

to be a part of the Nicki Barnes Crime Clique. My Father wrote me from time to time from different prisons. The ones I can recall is Attica and Clinton. I never treasured any of his writings or what he was saying to me, because he did not live with me and my Mother. I realized I didn't listen to what anyone told me. She used to say that "Billy everything I say to you goes in one ear and comes out the other." She said that so much I could see the words.

One day, I left my Dad's condo before it got dark. I noticed some folks on the side of the building gathering around.

They had a space that separated them from the crowd with a rope. On one side of the rope was a man behind two turntables, with numerous rectangles of machinery and a lamp, and wires connected to gigantic speakers. I can't recall the music being played, but it had to be something from Sugarhill. The beat was heavy and racy. I enjoyed the upbeat energy, and I did not want to leave. It felt like I belonged there, and I had to stay.

All of a sudden, the sounds stopped, and the crowd gave a big AWE! Later I would learn that the amplifier blew. I listened and watched the young men trouble shoot their equipment.

It was about to get dark, and I had to get home fast. I walked away, then I heard music come back on.... I was three blocks away, damn! I wished I could've stayed but I couldn't. I had to get home.

I Don't Know Why
She Was Proud Of Me

Mother was good on putting me on punishment for extended periods of time, that's probably why I desired a sibling. It got really lonely on the weekends, especially on Sundays, but I had just witnessed my first jam in the park. In the Bronx, New York. I was addicted to that vibe, in its purest form. Live from the Boogie Down Bronx, and I was hooked.

I learned quickly about important choices to make and the effects they can have. For instance, I had a bike, and I don't know why but it was yellow, and I hated it.

To the right of our building 2104 was a long steep hill, so one day, I decided to ride down the hill. My chain popped on my bike. I was traveling at an amazingly fast speed, and in front of me was a mailbox, and seven feet from it was a brick building. I had no way to stop other than choosing the mailbox to crash into or the brick building. I could've also continued to pick up speed onward towards the four-way traffic at the bottom of the hill which would probably end up in my death. So, I chose to crash into the mailbox.

I thought the impact would be less damaging than crashing into the hard brick structure. I rolled down the hill at top speed until I BANGED!!! into the mailbox, the bike was ruined. I hurled into the brick building anyway and received some minor scratches and scuff marks on my knees and elbows, nothing a little alcohol and a band aid couldn't fix; besides, I liked when the alcohol burnt in my open cuts and scrapes. I thought the alcohol was doing its job. I walked away with a yellow mangled bicycle.

I showed her what had happened. She looked at me shaking her head when I told her exactly what had happened. I didn't get a new bike, but I was glad it was irreparable. I didn't like the color and I wanted a blue mongoose BMX bike anyway.

This was a time period when I had seen HipHop in its purest form. I had learned about choices and consequences, but I also grew to learn about loneliness. I didn't have many friends as a boy if any. The kids were shielded by their parents, because kidnapping was at a high rate and pedophiles, we're on the prowl.

Some children could hardly come outside to play, only on Saturday's, after watching the karate show that came on at 3:00 PM on Channel 5. I think it was a show called drive in theatre. She gave me free roam outside the courtyard, so she could see me when I wasn't on a punishment.

I was hardheaded and I later on found out that this was a tactic she called giving me enough rope so I can hang myself. And as always, I took it a step further. I went across the street. I went down the block. I even went to my Father's house around the corner. I told her I saw him and his new family and everything. She was incredibly surprised when she found out where and how close my Father had lived. She would never get him on no child support because he was a hustler he stayed outside.

I Don't Know Why She Was Proud Of Me

She worried about where I was most of the time. When I was young, there was a commercial that came on television. It said, "It's 10:00. Do you know where your child is?"

I would be right there with her. She had me in check back then. We didn't have cell phones, so "I hope he is," or "I hope he didn't" were common statements for my Mommy to say.

School for me was a bore. It had always been to me. I recall my elementary days as a student. I felt unwelcomed, and I felt disrespected. I didn't know but probably in the second or third grade, I was feeling the injustice of being a student. Whose race was Black amongst the various cultures.

There were Asian students who would gather and play marbles in the dirt. It seemed like a complex game. I never got to know the name of the game or the children's names.

There was the Puerto Ricans, who communicated speaking in their language, and they stayed to themselves. I don't recall any other races in the school except for us. Yes, us, Black students; and of course, most of our teachers were white. I wasn't aware of this back then, but a lot of them were abusive, racist and prejudice.

I probably just smelled like piss. I was a dirt bomb little boy who pissed in the bed a lot, and I wore dirty socks with toe jam butter in between my toes and a fucked up haircut, and I wore dingy sweaters. No one was my friend and the teacher's flat out didn't care.

One teacher said she was only there for a check, and she would also say things like whether you learn or not, I still get paid. There was a science teacher that would call me a dummy. His name was Mr. Jones.

A female teacher would even beat students with five rulers taped together. It was called a magic wand. This disciplinary action was administered by a Black teacher, Her name was Ms. Bhase.

The teachers would often threaten me with phone calls to my home after school, in the evenings. It happened so often; I could time it. She would be making beef stew and rice with Jiffy cornbread for dinner while watching game shows and having a good ole time singing then the phone would ring. I would get scared because I knew Mom would transform into a mean person and her good mood would be ruined.

She would chastise me, then threaten me. She was going to tell her boyfriend. She loved that man but as I got older, I found out he didn't love her the same, and he had another girl on the other side of town. I named him The Dope Fiend Goon Bully Warren and he would whoop me.

There was this one girl around my age, and she had a big brother, and the girl would always get him to bully, harass, and pick on me. Every day in elementary school, he would push me around and put me in a headlock while

I Don't Know Why
She Was Proud Of Me

his sister smiled and watched. I now know that she liked me some kids find friendship in other people, but don't know how to express themselves.

This dude was a problem every day. On my way to school sometimes, I played hooky to prevent bumping into him and her to and from school.

One day, I was supposed to be in school, I cut class and went into my clubhouse in the abandoned building. I got bored being in there the entire day, so I went home, and told her that the teacher sent me home. She was furious, she took me back to the school and confronted the teacher.

The teacher told Mom with me standing next to her, that I had never been there. The teacher and Mom caught me in a lie, and I was in big trouble, so much trouble, that I was on punishment for the whole summer, and she told her boyfriend.

He was an abusive man towards my Mother, and others. His full name was Warren Bailey The Dope Fiend Goon Bully.

On another day, I ran into the girl and her brother, and he started pushing me around again. I was upset and I went home with tears in my eyes and sobbing uncontrollably. I ran to her. She was livid once again at me. She told me to go to my Father's house and talk to him. I went there sobbing and explaining to him about the harassment and bullying I had been encountering with the

I Don't Know Why
She Was proud Of Me

brother and his sister. I was fed up and now I told my Mom and my Dad.

I thought they were *gonna* get him for me. My Father wasn't having it. He made me take him to the bully and fight. This was the first time I had ever fought anyone. It was my Father, the boy, his sister, and a crowd of children he bullied as well. I did what came naturally.

I put my hands up and fought. I had no training other than watching Muhammad Ali and a lil bit of Sugar Ray Leonard on Wide World of Sports. This was a sports program that came on Channel 7.

"Put your hands up Billy and fuck him up!!! or else I'm *gonna* fuck you up!!" Father yelled!

I had never heard my Father yell profanities at me let alone call me Billy like that. I got nervous, but anxious. I wanted to show off my Ali shuffle, and my Sweet Sugar Ray boxing science. I admired so much from the champions I tried to emulate.

I wasn't trying to impress my Father, because I was mad at him for yelling and cussing at me. The children were entertained and surprised too as if they never heard someone use profanity towards a child while looking on spectating and enjoying the fight.

Needless to say, I fucked that dude up, I weaved, ducked, hit 'em with a right hook, then left hook, uppercut, then a right… he didn't hit me once, and that was it. My Father got in between us and broke it up and spared the boy anymore ass *whoopin'* and embarrassment. After that, his sister eventually became my lil girlfriend and her brother became my friend.

My Dad walked home with me. Proudly with his hand grasping my shoulder because his height was much greater than mines. I looked up at him in admiration for being my coach. I told my Mom of the encounter. I could tell she was glad that her version of Billy Lip came through. When she needed the basic father son natural intervention the most. I wished my Dad had stayed and became a family with us, but he didn't; he left and went around the corner. I had to be a family with The Dope Fiend Goon Bully Warren.

However, My life changed after that fight, as a boy in public school. I grew into popularity. The Asian kids noticed me, they gave head nods upon my arrival. The Spanish kids spoke in their own language, also giving head nods as to say hello or what's up. When I walked through the play area, the older fellas on the basketball court accepted me as a lil cool dude.

Word had spread around from the children that were watching the fight. I guess they told their older siblings, something that probably went like this. "Yo bro you know that lil dirty ass kid that be playing in the dirt, well he beat so and so up so bad, his dad had to jump in and stop the fight yo! You should've been there bro."

Yeah, rumor spread around, and all the girls smiled at me, and the boys ice grilled me, as if they wanted or wouldn't mind challenging me to a fight. I automatically gained confidence and more swagger as a kid.

I had gained respect in those streets on Aqueduct Avenue as a lil man. This was my first exposure to being good in the hood. I loved being cool and not a cornball, plus I was the son of Big Billy Lip. I couldn't be a sucker either.

Meanwhile at home, we had to wash our clothes by hand still and hang them on the shower rails or on the heater with all that work. I just rocked my clothes dirty most of the time. I could never forget the smell of ironing dirty clothes. It smells like hot steam coming from the grate on the ground of New York City sidewalks.

I got into writing graffiti, my name was Willie Rock, and I practiced writing letters and trying to create graffiti characters for years. I would continue to be affected by these elements of HipHop unknowingly still watching the guys set up their equipment, and jam in the park. I'd imagine myself as the guy who was on the microphone, and I'd become M.C. Willie Rock.

I became confident and like a sponge, I soaked up all my environment had to offer, I also had a raggedy one or two lil boys with me plus the guy I beat up. I had a lil crew.

We went to Fordham Road and stole some fruit from the fruit stand. We didn't intend on doing it. It was just a stupid kid's impulse. In the midst of so-called thievery, I attempted to run across a busy up the hill six lane road. This was a terribly busy road that have curves and hills where vehicles traveled at least 35 to 40 mph up it and down, speeding, you name it. All of us grabbed fruit one after the other and ran across the busy roadway.

We just took some red delicious apples and maybe an orange or two. They all ran across the street dodging cars like it was a football drill. It was my turn, I grabbed my fruit and attempted to run through the ongoing traffic and SMACK! I got hit by a sedan.

I flipped up in the air two times and landed flat on my face! I was bleeding from my mouth, my front tooth was cracked in half, and I was also scraped and scuffed but I survived. They called her, and I spent a lot of time at home being on a punishment while I was healing.

She knew I was attracted to the streets. It hurt me to watch outside the window staring at a brick wall. If you look down, you can see the basement. No action ever went down there. Everything happened at the front window where I could be monitored. I'd look from there and see people coming and going from wherever.

I loved the moments I got to watch television with her. I did not have a television in my room at this time.

I had to watch what she put on in her bedroom. Shows such as Dynasty, I love Lucy, Gilligan's Island, The Brady Bunch, The Love Boat, All My Children, Barney Miller, General Hospital, Mission Impossible, and Kojak.

I hated watching Westside Story. That was one of her favorite musicals. She loved Bing Crosby, Fred Astaire, etc. I liked the gangster films she watched starring James Cagney and Humphrey Bogard, Jane Kelly, Clint Eastwood, Charles Bronson and Westerns like Bonanza and The Magnificent Seven with Charleston Heston and Kathryn Hepburn. These were the shows and the actors I was exposed to as a kid. I spent many summers on punishment watching Soap Operas with my Mom, suspensions from school and all.

I was a kid that got up early and watched Channel 13. Where you'd see educational shows. I would learn English, math, social skills, science, writing and reading; actually, it was like today online studying.

Davey and Goliath was a series I watched too. It informed you about Christianity by using Claymation characters, and then there was always the Jimmy Swaggart Program. He is a television evangelist. He was the first Preacher I had seen on television talking about God.

Every Saturday, the kids used to come outside in front of the building and practice there karate skills; they'd learn from watching the kung fu flicks on Channel 5 at 3:00 PM. I was serious about my karate. I liked the snake style, and made the sound effects with my mouth, attempting to copy what I saw and heard on TV.

Another experience I can remember is, one day me and a girl was playing in the hallway, she was doing her thing jumping rope and I was doing mine running around, then I started jumping from the stairs. She told me the higher I jumped she would give me a kiss. I jumped three at a time and received kisses. This was my first interaction with a girl showing me affection.

I liked it, so I kept doing it, and ended up jumping down whole flights of stairs, for more kisses. She was a fresh lil girl, and I was a young boy who liked girls.

She was nice and I liked her big sister too. I liked all the women and young ladies that I saw on television, Captain Stuben's daughter from the love boat, Thelma from Good Times, Lieutenant Uhura from Star Trek, all the women from Charlie's Angels, and all of the ladies from the show Three's Company. I even had a crush on Crystal Carrington from Dynasty.

I was a boy with a man size appetite for the ladies, and I wasn't exposed to anythin-rated yet. I was curious about everything. My Mother noticed this about me and bought me an encyclopedia set with a bookshelf that housed the volumes. In it was age appropriate pictures, maps, explanations, and definitions, on everything my impressionable mind could absorb at the time.

I recall Mom having her own little library. She had books such as Alex Haley's "Roots," the Dictionary, some romance novels that didn't get my interest, medical books that seemed too advanced for me, but I still attempted to read them, especially the one by Alex Haley. The book "Roots" became a movie and aired on television a lot, so I was already familiar with the story. I was weak in math, and I knew I had to master telling time and counting money.

I Don't Know Why She Was proud Of Me

When I'd go to the store, I'd see folks after paying for their purchases say keep the change. I'd emulate them and buy potato chips, cookies, and a soda with a five-dollar bill, given to me by my uncle or one of my Mother's friends.

One day I told the store attendant to keep the change, I could sense I was making a costly mistake, cause I was trying to be grown. The attendant would pause, as if to say, "Are you sure?" And I'd be like, "Yeah," like lil dumb ass, trying to act like a big shot. He would also be delighted at me not knowing how to count money. I left feeling like I jerked myself unknowingly. She would know how much money I had, and she would get the change back. She would often ask why I needed more money when I was just given a $10 here, and a $5 there.

I was just copying folks saying keep the change. I got tired of not knowing about cash and change. I stopped saying keep the change too, so in school I paid attention and studied hard about counting money and telling time. It was to my detriment and survival.

I learned a lot from the short episodes of School House Rock on Channel 7. Politics, government, and social issues, they used to teach through songs, which was generally jazzy and bluesy, and catchy. I learned science and multiplication from episodes of 3, 2, 1 Contact on PBS Channel 13 and social skills watching episodes of Sesame Street.

I Don't Know Why
She Was Proud Of Me

While being on punishment or left home alone, kids get into things. As I stated before, there were things hidden from me at my house and I went through anything and everywhere when Mom wasn't home.

I eventually found her boyfriend's Playboy Penthouse books, and some other reading material that wasn't kid appropriate. I even found a gun in one drawer and bullets in another, but I still found more interest in reading those encyclopedias, every one of them. It was like twenty-eight of them fully illustrated, colorful and designed for easy reading.

It puzzled me on how many words began with Z at that time there weren't many. She tried to be careful not to expose me to adult situations. She always said watch your mouth when grown folks are talking or excuse me from the room when she was with company. When I couldn't be dismissed while we were visiting her friends, they would speak in a language like the DaSEFx iggedy rap style. The grownups called it Pig Latin. I was a young kid growing up out of the 70s into the 80s as a child.

Me and the other children were dirt poor. We'd find joysticks in the rubble and imagine we were playing Atari with no console. I wore the unstylish, cheap stuff. A lot of poor kids grew up wearing clothing from Mays, Conway, Alexander's and even Woolworth because many of us Black kids in New York City grew up in poverty. These were stores similar to what you see now that sells the latest cheap versions of high-end clothing. I hadn't had a pair of Nike's yet. I didn't have any Pony Converse,

I Don't Know Why
She Was proud Of Me

Puma or Pro Keds shoes either. I had sneakers from a store called Fayva, and they were even knock offs. I was a child, and I wanted a pair of karate shoes like Bruce Lee and many martial artists I've seen on Channel 5.

One day my exposure to the Bronx was over. Mom got an apartment back home. In my birthplace Manhattan, The Village of Harlem. Home of Doug E. Fresh, George Carlin, Sammy Davis Jr. Cam'ron Marcus Garvey, and actor/choreographer/singer the beautiful Teyana Taylor. Over there, you'd better not be slipping when it comes to clothing, footwear, haircuts, food, or glasses. The snaps you'd receive could bring you to tears for years if you were weak. But, if you were witty, funny, and edgy, you'd clap back and become popular. Or you could always get fresh and make those folks eat their words.

Everyone likes a strong comeback, and everyone loved the underdog. Harlem was different from the Bronx The birthplace of HipHop, home of DJ Scott La Rock, The New York Yankees, and the best pizza in the world.

I fell deeply in love with comic books, too, especially the ones with the Los Angeles Lakers on the back. That was the only part of the comic book, where people who looked like me were at. I collected them from a hustle I had. My collection grew to about three deep dresser drawers full of comic books.

I created this hustle because I couldn't pack bags well at the supermarket, like the rest of the kids. So, I carried the customers' bags, and I received tips. I had a paper route situation, where I'd go to the store and get the newspaper for folks and receive tips. I also had a Kool-Aid stand which didn't last long.

I foolishly traded all of my comics for a cheap watch that I found interesting because it had a tachometer and it displayed the days of the week, and it had an alarm, and calculator. It was a Casio Databank knock off I'd later learned. This wouldn't be the first stupid thing I did.

I had no idea of value, business, or hard work and how it pays off. I had no one to teach me that I was truly not thinking like a boss in my younger years, I hustled backwards. Could this not knowing anything be the result of not having a strong father figure in the house? I had my Uncle, but he had his own son and daughter issues. When Warren the Dope Fiend Goon Bully found out what I did with my comics he looked at me like I was stupid.

My Father was absent for a prolonged period of time at this point in my life. Later on, I found out he had gone to jail. He wrote me letters from prison, and she would give them to me, but I was too young to understand the seriousness of being incarcerated. I was introduced to the street life, and this was Harlem. I had mad fun.

The first time I witnessed death was when my friend's big brother had gotten killed. She loved him and he was gone forever. He may have only been sixteen. She was also a fast and fresh little girl. Everyone liked her and talked about her.

I Don't Know Why She Was proud Of Me

She knocked on my door one day, and I answered it before my Mother could hear it travel to the back of the apartment, where her room was. It was her Becky, as I looked through the peep hole. I opened the door, she smiled and asked if she could borrow some sugar? I wondered to myself in those seconds, why would she travel all the way from the next building where she lived, then walk six flights up to my apartment and be asking for sugar. I could tell she was incredibly sad because her brother had just gotten killed, as I gazed into her pretty young eyes. She gave me a long tongue kiss, while I held the door open. I didn't let her in the house. I was a virgin, unaware of anything sexual just kissing.

The demographic population in Harlem had mostly Black people living there. A lot of positive people, Black power, culture, and it was beautiful, exciting, fresh, and alive. This was a time when soda and milk would get delivered to your stoop in Harlem. One cent could buy you lots of candy.

It was this same time when Grandmaster Flash and Furious Five was the best Rap group and Kurtis Blow was the King of HipHop. He was GQ and clean cut. My uncle even bought his single "The breaks." These guys were Fly to me.

Kurtis Blow is from Harlem. He is Rap's first superstar. He was the first King of Rap. The B. Fats "Woppit" record had the city on fire. I think it was conceived from the projects of Drew Hamilton on 144th Street on 7th Avenue.

I Don't Know Why She Was Proud Of Me

Teddy Riley's early works, with the classical Two Rap's New Generation, Doug E. Fresh, The Get Fresh Crew, with Slick Rick had made a grand impact throughout the world with their single "The Show." The Luv Bug Starski you *gotta* believe single heated the Harlem streets up along with Donald Dee's groove. D.J. Hollywood's greatest hits certified The Harlem Sound at that time. The Rooftop crew, with D.J. Brucie B and The Mix King Ron -G from 155th Street. MasterDon and The Death Committee's addictive sound gave birth to Master P from New Orleans fame. These were some of my neighborhood Harlem Heroes. This is what's known as the golden era of Harlem HipHop.

Mr. Magic, Kool D.J. Red Alert, and D.J. Chuck Chillout had already began to heat up the FM airwaves. House and Freestyle music from Bronx had seeped into the culture too.

I had some growing up to do some learning and exploring. I was a young boy, still curious, dirty, and full of energy and creativity. I've been here before as a toddler, an infant. I was born in Harlem Hospital and so was my whole family. We were born Harlemites.

I was excited to be in an environment full of endless odysseys and adventures. I've seen some kids there before, because of my visits, with my Mom's friends. She used to take me almost everywhere she went.

I didn't like it because there were no cool kids for me to play with. There were some neighbors, a mother with

I Don't Know Why She Was Proud Of Me

three boys and a girl. The mother was heavyset and there was no father figure around. The sister was cool. She stayed to herself guarded by everyone, I didn't like her. They went to a church in the middle of the block on 145th Street. As a child and being from Harlem you quickly adapt to who's cool and who's not.

The church boys with the one sister wasn't the cool crowd. Once I figured that out, I distanced myself. The church kids felt like I had flat out left them for another group of kids. I didn't care. I wanted to play and have fun. They all seemed like servants to their mom, and they didn't dress nor act like the other kids playing basketball, chilling, and running around. They wore church clothes to go outside and play.

I quickly got into the mix of the children who played tag, freeze tag super freeze tag Skelly's, and redlight green light 1, 2, 3. There was also a game the fresh lil children played called run, catch and kiss.

My Uncle Gerald bought me a leather V bomber jacket and some pinstriped Lees. He made me fresh. I was well mannered compliments of my Mother, so when I got around other kid's parents, they took a liking to me. I was very respectful, and aware of my surroundings.

We lived on the top floor, six flights of stairs within the tenement building. I'd run up and down those stairs in 10 seconds, grocery shopping was a workout especially with six to eight bags real heavy ones too.

I Don't Know Why
She Was Proud Of Me

Shopping carts was a necessity. We didn't have one. We used the market shopping cart to take the groceries home then I had to bring the cart back to the market. This was a time in my life when I was a kid. I was innocent and a sponge. I learned as I saw things. I learned that if you wanted anything you had to work hard for it. And only the strong survived. There was a saying, closed mouths don't get fed. I was hungry and far from lazy.

I wanted more and the treasures of HipHop was all around me. There was a roller-skating rink called The Rooftop. There was 125th Street where everyone who loved the HipHop culture came to get fly. There was also jams in the parks, and festivals which gave The Harlemites a sense of unity, pride, and hope while being Black.

Kid Capri mixtapes were sold in front of the supermarket where we lived. He was one of the first D.J.'s that I heard pioneer a style of mixing and scratching while controlling the crowd. There were others before him, but this was at the time of Rap's new generation.

I was very hands on in the community. We had four libraries within a 10-block radius. There were at least one basketball court on every block, whether makeshift or a public park. We had three swimming pools within the community. One was at the Bath House on 135th Street, and the second was private invites only. This was in "Esplanade Gardens." These luxury buildings ran from 145th to 149th Street. Then there was the community pool on Bradhurst and 145th Street.

I Don't Know Why
She Was proud Of Me

We had so much fun there, but afterwards you'd get so hungry and thirsty. Sometimes we didn't have anything to eat; after leaving the pool. It was hot and when the fun was over, you'd be dehydrated and starving. Some kids would pack bags for tips and then buy Chinese food, or pizza from Willie's. There was also Willie's Burgers, a delicious hamburger spot on the side of 145th Street and 8th Avenue.

One thing about Willie's is that you had to have at least $3.00 for a burger. Back then things were cheaper. You could stretch $3.00. You could buy a $1.00 spice ham and cheese hero or sub. We called large sandwiches hero's uptown. You could get a $0.50 Sunnydale to drink, a pack of Little Debbie cookies for $0.25 and $0.25 worth of penny candy. You would still have money left over. Back then this was called loose change, and you could use it to make phone calls. This was a time when you had to pay to use a phone, cellphones was a dream back then.

Everything we do today was a dream back then, film had to be developed, you couldn't just use your phone to take pictures. Information was received by snail mail, or you had to get it from a physical place called a library. There were many throughout the city just a stroll away.

Many of the kids ate bags upon bags of penny candy. The fruit and healthy options in the hood got ignored. I ate candy all the time. I loved eating candy coated apples sprinkled with coconut dust on top. I did not brush my teeth twice a day, nor did I use dental floss, so I ended up having cavities and needing oral surgeries as a teen and when I got older.

It also didn't help that I had a broken front tooth for years due to me getting hit by that car and falling on my face; that was equivalent to having an open wound in my mouth. It got infected, and I had to have it removed, and replaced with a cap.

Mommy had developed a drinking problem of some sort; but she still tried to instill good parenting skills within me, I was just hard headed and I couldn't listen to anything she said. Her words were truly going in one ear and out the other. My young mind was elsewhere. I may have driven her to heavier drinking, but still she had to get focused. She was tough on me, and I respected her authority. One time when she was scolding me, I thought she was *gonna* slap me, so I threw up my hands to block her strikes, but she thought I was trying to raise my hands in a fighting stance toward her. She went upside my head all the way down our long hallway.

I would never think of going against her at any moment, but I guess she had to make it known by saying, "I brought you into this world and I'll take you out." She nipped that in the bud, really quick.

As I said before, I had no responsible father figure in the home, except for Warren The Dope Fiend Goon Bully. He smoked Marlboro and wore a headband. I guess that was to keep sweat from pouring in his eyes, while he biked to Mosholu Parkway, in the Bronx where he worked.

He was a beast. He was a nightmare walking as far as I could see. He had no feminine tendencies. He resembled Teddy Pendergrass. He carried a big 007 knife on his belt, to stab anyone, and whoever he felt was a threat, not to mention as I said earlier, he had an unloaded thirty-eight in Mom's dresser drawer. The bullets were in another drawer. I scurried through her room every now and then when I got bored.

He had gruff in his voice and veins poked out of his hands and arms. He had a hairy chest, and he wore a silver chain that didn't dangle. His genuine masculine presence would have my Mother's alcoholic friends witnessing an evil general on deck. They saluted.

He came through the foyer of the tenement building where they partied and conversed with slurry word communication. He drank their pints and beer and the convos got slower and awkward. Then he ordered her upstairs and argued to the top floor. He had his own key and opened the door. We went inside. I was the last person to close the door. I could hear his yelling and my Mother responding standing up for herself. I tried to intervene, but my Mother ordered me to go to my room.

We are from the streets, and I believe, my Mother and Uncle didn't approve of the image portrayed as Jesus being white. Mom didn't expose me to Christianity. I think she said she was Catholic.

I Don't Know Why
She Was Proud Of Me

After a while, all the church going kids mothers refrained there kids from playing with me, because by this time, I hung with the rowdy kids. The kids that had that HipHop feel to them and movements. The ones who wore Soda Club leathers and high-top spot-bilt sneakers. The Party People in the house Sayyy HO! The kind of people I became a store boy for some of the dudes named Rome, Blatz, and Don Woo. These guys were hustlers and Blatz was the boss. These guys sold dope and a whole lot of it, right around the corner from my block. I was given a breakfast of my choice or whatever they ordered I ordered. This breakfast consisted of pancakes, cheese eggs and beef sausage cooked well done.

The restaurants we ordered from were either Reliables/Copelands or Sandra's. These were restaurants in Harlem where The Hustlers ate at and left big tips for the cooks and servers. I took A Touch of Class car service. whenever I went up the hill to Copelands/Reliables. Back and forth and received a $20.00 tip and an easy two store runs equal a $40.00 tip. I got comic book money. Yeah, this was the 80s, and parents did not understand the music, the slang, nor the fashion.

Oftentimes, they would attempt to bully me and cave in my chest, just messing around that's how they weeded out who was soft and who had heart. They had to stop me from throwing bottles and getting back up after having my chest caved in and knocked me down. There was also this other young kid who used to take the punches like it was nothing and walk away, he was different. His name was Jeze. I had this insight on certain people, I could tell who souls were in it and whose weren't. I could feel the passion for those who really was about that life, and some weren't meant for hustling. They should've stayed in school.

I took in the suspense and danger around me as I inserted myself around the drug dealers and criminals. This was an active dope spot. The drug dealers stamped whatever was popular on the bags of dope they sold. This particular brand was called New Edition worth $25.00 a bag.

I didn't grasp the big picture of this reality. If I were to get caught by detectives or murdered, at this point, I didn't give a fuck. My mind was juvenile. I thought I was slick. I knew I had to be on the lookout for folks that would tell my Mother where I hung out. I was shocked at how she found out where I was. I figured if I were somewhere I wasn't supposed to be and this person was buying dope, they wouldn't tell on me, but they did. It was Derek's mom, but I denied it when confronted by my Mother.

It sounded something like this "Billy, I don't want you around the corner where they be selling them drugs."

And I'd be like, "I won't I just be waiting for my friend."

And she be like, "Friend who?"

I Don't Know Why
She Was Proud Of Me

And I say some bogus name like, "My man Paul, Kev, and Rod."

And she'd be like, "Yeah right you think I'm stupid WILLIAM!"

Derek and his parents lived on the same floor as me but in a different building. His mother looked like a Nubian goddess. She wore a head wrap, at times and needed bifocals to see. Sometimes she let her long black dreads hang, as I recall her coming to the front door, when I knocked on her door to see if Derek could come outside to play. Her boyfriend would answer the door at times too. He was a chump for a boyfriend to her. I sensed her boyfriend was a sucker, He would later get swept up in the nearing crack wave that hit all major ghettos and he probably introduced my friend's mom to the powerful drug ... now that I think back.

My Mother had no idea I was ducking the truancy patrol unit that would travel throughout the city picking up kids and driving them to the police precinct and calling their schools and parents to pick them up.

A girl trio from the Bronx named Expose ran the air waves, The Petshop Boys, The Rapping Duke, Glen Jones, and of course Michael Jackson provided the soundtrack back then. Harlem was a different village or place.

You'd hardly ever saw white people come passed 96th Street on the number three train. They would not ride passed 59th Street on the D or A train. Only if the

I Don't Know Why She Was Proud Of Me

Yankees were playing. I will say this, some white people would come into the neighborhood for other reasons.

The neighborhoods where full of abandoned vacant buildings one after another. There were little children looking dingy, with long goose raggedy coats on playing in rubble or snow. Making things from spare parts, homemade bicycles from scraps in the garbage or empty lots.

There was the neighborhood junk dealer where he'd have a shop with all kinds of forgotten and minor broken pieces of equipment, radios, VCR movies, tape recorders, and he repaired bikes and fixed flats.

I used to buy a patch kit and fix my own bike and buy brakes for it. He'd have comic books and I attempted to rebuild my collection. He also sold jewelry at times. I was lucky I had a Nintendo R.O.B but I didn't have the console. We had a black and white TV for a while, so I could hardly hook anything up to my television without an adapter.

Somehow two young white guys would come through knocking on doors to talk about Jesus Christ. It was the guys from The Church of Latter-Day Saints. Later on in life, my kids would think one of them looked like Jim Carrey.

We were young growing up. We grew aware of the many injustices and unfair treatment white people have done to Black folks in the United States of America and throughout slavery from Jim Crow to the present. So, in the mid to late 70s and 80s, those Black teenagers gained knowledge of self-awareness and the white man was considered the Devil.

My Mom didn't discuss anything about race or society as a whole with me. She allowed me to have the experiences and figure it out on my own. Plus, after reading the book entitled "Roots," it gave me more of our experiences as a Black race of people. The book was made into a miniseries.

The Church and God was always important to me. I love God, Jesus, and Holy Spirit. One of the church kids told me if I wanted a girlfriend, I could find one in church. He was not lying. His church was a mile away. I put on my lil' cheap church clothes and went to the house of the Lord. Even though I went to get girls, I still got the message.

She knew there was something different about me besides the fact that I was changing. I was spending more time outside. I would get in trouble at school, as always and everyone could hear my Mother's boyfriend yelling out my name up and down the block "BILLY!!!!"

I'd hide under cars or run at top speed a block away. One time he tried to track me down, I mean for real like he went in the backyard through the abandoned buildings, and everything. But he was not as fast as me. He didn't know the pathways through the abandoned apartments within the vacant buildings like me.

I Don't Know Why
She Was proud Of Me

Warren was out of control. I saw him punch and beat his own mother. She was a frail old woman, and I heard the punches being absorbed by her little body. He'd question folks, kids, and anyone. "Did you see Billy?" The people would be like, "No…." Because they didn't know Billy. I had a street name, and it was "King Amperck" AMPE for short.

There was no snitching amongst the group of kids I ran with. We were the Get Busy Boys, and we were having fun being young Black and clueless. We didn't understand drugs kill and destroy communities, and I didn't understand that going to jail was a terrible thing.

Watching how my Father made doing jail bids look easy, there was hardly any positive role models for me to look up to. All we had were our mom's raising boys to men. There were a few exceptions amongst our families. You would get a glimpse of households where there were two parents present and what that looked like was a hard-working father, with a nice-looking mother.

The fathers would work all day and the moms coming in looking like party girls worn out. Or a mother in her role as a housewife and the father was tired and overworked.

While I stressed her out every time, she still went to parent-teachers' night. I can swear by it that the teachers had no good news for my Mom. After the meeting, I could see my Mom coming home looking exhausted, and annoyed by what teachers had told her about me. It was

I Don't Know Why She Was Proud Of Me

the same feeling I got when I had problems in elementary school in the Bronx. This was *gonna* be a long night. She would discuss it with her boyfriend; and he would whip my ass with a thick black belt.

He was a terrible man. His hands weren't swollen from using needles; he must've injected in other areas, because he was big and intimidating. He did not have a dope fiend appearance, but you would see him nodding off slipping from time to time.

I knew what was up because I told you I snooped around my Mother's room. I saw a syringe, spoon, aluminum foil and so on. He was bad to my Mother, and I think he used to take her food stamps and welfare money.

One time he beat my Mother really bad. I saw him carry her to the tub to have her soak. She was crying and mumbling, "Why you keep doing this to me…?" He was talking in a please forgive me manner, incredibly low and kind of slurry with his words.

Realistically, I wasn't totally captured by the streets, yet I was just a lil kid just getting into junior high school. I hadn't even used a lot of profanity yet nor had I drunk a beer or started dating. I didn't want to shoot Warren The Dope Fiend Goon Bully, although he deserved it. He needed to go.

Warren had one brother and a sister. The men in their family beat the women. His sister felt deep sorrow for my Mother and her mother. His brother used to beat his kids

I Don't Know Why
She Was proud Of Me

with extension cords, and their bodies showed welts like tiger stripes.

Nowadays, that abuse would be grounds for prison. However, these are the early influences of men. I had to look up to as a child. I couldn't take the ill-treatment any longer. The mental abuse, neglect, and torture Mommy and I was subjected to was unbearable. The terror and also the lies he was telling her because he was a cheater too. He once took me to his other chick's house.

I was young but not stupid. He had a pair of Fisher speakers at our house that I admired very much, and then they disappeared. This place he took me too was his other chick's house. Those same speakers were there too.

I could feel my Mom's pain. I felt disappointed in him. She loved and trusted him. I may not have been a threat to him or even had the power to stop him, but this was enough to call my big gun my Daddy Billy Lip. After I listened to her crying and whimpering, I had had enough!

I headed to the streets right where my Dad would be on the corner or around the corner to Bradhurst Avenue on 147th Street. There, I saw my Father talking to some woman. He had his fitted cap to the side, and he had on a black Adidas® jacket with the big logo on the back of it and another small logo on the front. He would let me wear it sometimes.

I explained to my Father what was going on inside of my house. He looked at me in disbelief. He asked me,

I Don't Know Why
She Was Proud Of Me

"Why didn't you tell me about this sooner? Is he still over there?"

I said, "Yes.

"He put her in the tub. She was hurt and crying. He was punching her."

My Father told the lady he'd be right back. He adjusted his pistol he had tucked in his Levi's, pulled over his BVD T-shirt and we began to walk down 7th Avenue towards my apartment on 145th Street. When we got there, he started banging on the door BOOM! BOOM! BOOM!

My Father said, "Open this fuckn' door nga!"

We heard noises from behind the door, so my Dad impatiently kicked the door, BAMM! BAMM! with two kicks. There he was Warren The Dope Fiend Goon Bully standing in the hallway with his 007 knife in his hand.

My Father quickly moved his hand and gun butted him as we entered the corridor. Warren the Dope Fiend Goon Bully staggered back away from the door grabbing his head.

Blood started streaming down his face and swelling started to appear on his forehead. My Dad cocked his gun and aimed it at The Dope Fiend Goon Bully, and said, "Knife to a gunfight nga really?"

I was hyped and cheering my Dad on like when he made me fight the bully in the Bronx. I was jumping up and down as if I were saying, *fuck em up dad*.

I Don't Know Why
She Was proud Of Me

She leaped out of the tub dripping wet and stood in between them and said, "Billy Don't do it." talking directly to my Dad.

In my mind, I was thinking, *Dad Do It*! But then I quickly grabbed her robe which hung behind the bathroom door and put it over her dripping wet bruised body. Because she was standing in between them naked.

My dad told Warren in a stern threatening masculine tone, "If you ever touch my son or Patty again.... She *ain't gonna* be able to save you. Ya knife to a gun fight bringing ass nga!" and then he left.

Warren and my Mother were standing there. I left with my Father. He looked so cool. I was like, "You handled that, Daddy!" I was proud, and I looked up to my Father in a way.

As we walked down the street; he told me never put your hands on a woman. I don't care what she does, protect yourself, but don't ever slap, punch, or kick a woman then he asked me, "Do you understand that, Billy?"

I said, "Yes, Daddy." and we dapped and embraced one another.

He'd ask me, "You got some money, Billy?" and usually I'd say no. Then he'd give me some money. I'd go and buy some candy apples and comic books.

I Don't Know Why She Was Proud Of Me

Later on, that night when I came home, she was asleep in her room. I went over to her bed and kissed her forehead and whispered, "I love you."

She mumbled back sleepily, "Love you too Billy. Goodnight."

I went to my bedroom and cut on the DNA and Hank Love HipHop radio show. It was 2:00 A.M., and things were well, for now.

I always had a thing for females. I liked the tone of their voices and their hair. I was attracted to their body language, and the way they looked in their clothing. These girls were fast and so was the fellas. The Adina Howard Freak Like Me was the anthem and the vibez.

I can recall some of the Get Busy Boys playing hooky having parties when their mom went to work. These were the around the way girls. They wore Reeboks® and some girls wore the fake Reeboks which was called In Actions. And then there were the Get Busy Girls. These young women were about their schoolwork, career goals, and getting to the next level.

Shout out to my stepsister Shiba. She was one of the first to have an apartment on Park Avenue and secured her future.

We were leaving the dope era and entering the crack era. Game rooms/arcades were a front for the drug dealers, or scramblers is what we called them back then. They sold cocaine jumbo vials and weed in the back of the establishment. Cell phone charging stations, coffee shops, fine eateries, street gardens, two car garages, nice pathways, and friendly neighbors, was not today's version of Harlem, or any version of the metropolitan area of New York in those days.

It could be fog settling throughout the drug infested Village of Harlem. Miles of burnt-out city blocks. Children throughout the Village of Harlem still playing in the abandoned school on 147th and 148th Street. Lincoln town cars, Porche's and custom white, red, or black BMW M3s parked in front of sketchy tenement buildings.

Piss under the stairs, where the young homeless lurked, crackheads smoking their rocks. Stick up kids holding family members for ransom, and honest working folk just enjoying being a Harlemite.

Broken crack stems littered the streets. We regulated our homes no beaming up to Scottie or smoking rocks in our buildings where we lived. I became a regulator, but one day someone pulled a big pump shotgun out on me like lil nga what!

I never saw this guy or girl again. I should've been more scared, because a cool cat like me lost one of his nine lives that day. I continued to walk through a cloud of angel dust every morning; passed the garbage cans and luxury cars getting washed by the curb. This version of Harlem was a hustler's wonderland. It was intense, exciting, and dangerous. I still hadn't drunk or smoked yet.

I Don't Know Why She Was Proud Of Me

HipHop was thriving, and the first record I ever purchased was Washington DC's own Chuck Brown. The father of Go Go's Bustin Loose.

She never smoked cocaine or crack. Thank God, but she did enjoy her other Bacardi and Winston cigarettes, and she had started to drink more water too. She wasn't a wine drinker. She was doing her best as a single mom. There were precious moments we shared.

When New Years came around, it was an exciting time. We'd make sure we were together and got hats, noise makers, horns, then countdown with the New Years Rocking Eve with Dick Clark.

Our neighbor Sam used to come by after the ball dropped and ask me to walk through his front door. I'd be sipping on that apple cider while they drank that Bacardi Dark. She was just adjusting to being in her mid-30s; it wasn't easy.

We we're no stranger to government cheese, which came in the rectangle box. The flour and other things in a black and white canister. Times could get hard, and I had to step my game up as the lil man of the house.

I cleaned the house as I did when I was younger and cooked her breakfast. We could not afford going to the laundromat, so as I mentioned earlier, we washed our clothes by hand. In this particular apartment our bedrooms both faced the back of the building.

I Don't Know Why
She Was proud Of Me

She attempted to go to nursing school but couldn't take the part about drawing blood. It made her cringe, so she just got her certificate and never pursued that career. She worked for the Park's Department for some time while I enjoyed being in middle school.

I was in full HipHop mode now and I admired The Kings from Queens Run DMC and Jam Master Jay. While starting to become a bigger problem for her, I was getting worst with my behavior. I was becoming a product of my environment.

As usual she would be in the kitchen singing and dancing swinging herself around, while listening to Peabo Bryson's song, "I'm So Into You." She'd often grab my face and sing to me, or grab my hands, and we'd dance together.

She'd try to teach me how to dance with a lady. I'd be stepping on her toes trying to keep up and she'd be dodging my feet from stepping on hers, while still holding me and steering me into the dance.

The Dope Fiend Goon Bully Warren died from a drug overdose. His Brother died two weeks later. Their Dad died too, and they all should be burning in hell. Weights were lifted off of my Mother's shoulders.

I often would drift off in thought about things I've seen and gone through. So, one day I walked into the street, and I was struck by a car again; thinking about the first time I had gotten hit by that other car on Fordham Road. This time I didn't get flipped up in the air and land

I Don't Know Why
She Was Proud Of Me

on my face. It was just a lil scrape. I was okay. I didn't even need an ambulance.

The next day, my friends and I cut school. We were into graffiti, girls snapping, Run DMC, LL Cool J, and the young R&B group New Edition. The rap music had an effect on the youth. Some of the songs described our emotions, things that was going on in our homes, Black communities, and our deep dark side that was within Street NGZ. I was culture shocked and loved NWA's lyrics "Fuck The Police," "Bitches Ain't Shit," "We Want Eazy," and "Straight Out of Compton."

I didn't gravitate towards the message on their song "Express Yourself" because I was surrounded by all the Black Power references from The Schomburg Library which I frequented often.

The 125th Mart 125 vender experiences, the vendors on the sides of the streets. The historical events inside the stores. Such rich sparkling cases of mixtapes. I was surprised at the direction HipHop was going in. It was a surge of drug selling tales in rap.

The way I grew up and was raised it sounded like it was snitching on wax if you unveiled your hustle scheme, and your crew's inner dealings. But that's the culture and I lived my lyrics by age twenty.

I had witnessed firsthand the shadowy world called Harlem. I would watch the sun rise over Yankee stadium looking above the roof of the tenement building. I would feel the energy of nightfall and the rhythm of

I Don't Know Why She Was Proud Of Me

hand-to-hand sales throughout the morning; whether legal or illegal.

You could sell cups of Kool-Aid near the steel garbage cans, with matching lids, and they'd buy it. New York City always had its rat and roaches' population. This was a rotten apple. The police officers were rotten.

One precinct was called The Dirty 30 Lawyers who were corrupt where wrongful convictions and undercover drug deals were being done. Injustices across the board were publicized on the front page of the Daily News. The New York Post from the Central Park jogger, to Larry Davis from Eleanor bumpers to the murder of Yusef Hawkins, the sodomizing of Amadou Diallo, the cannibalistic Jefferey Dahmer. Train shootings were done by Bernard Getz an eastside rapist / a westside rapist.

The burning of an entire night club with people trapped inside of it in the Bronx. This fire was set by a jealous boyfriend. My friend's sister died and many others in The Happy Land Social Club fire in the Bronx.

The slaying of Sean Bell, a man who was finishing his bachelor party and was to be married the next day. He was slayed innocently by police in New York City.

Columbia University where people got trampled over and died. There was also antics that made headlines bought by Donald Dump, a native New Yorker who some rappers metaphorically championed because of his wealth and play boyish image.

I Don't Know Why She Was Proud Of Me

The assassination of Malcolm X was done here, and President Bill Clinton had an office in Harlem. Then the Fall of the skyline. The 911 attack. The fall of The Twin Towers and The World Trade Center. These were some of the most horrific times in the history of New York and Harlem.

You could feel the good times when The African American Day Parade was celebrated annually in Harlem. All the communities would get together and have floats, radio personalities and television personalities would attend. Politicians and celebrities would participate, walking from 110th Street on 7th Avenue passing 140th Street and beyond.

There would be fairs and events throughout New York City and Harlem that would make you proud to be a New Yorker. This was our home, The Big Apple. NYC where HipHop and Rap was created. We represented with Yankee baseball caps, Met's hats, and New York Knick caps. We have a style and HipHop was duplicated and imitated throughout the world.

This was a time when white men preferred white women with flat asses and big breasts. They referred to fully developed Black women as Jungle Bunny's with jungle booty's, and fat shaming a full-figured thick woman's body.

No matter the race, amongst all this madness and happiness, I met Frank. He was the other kid the dope dealers would try to cave in his chest, and they would practically hurt their hands, Frank loved milk; just like I loved candy. The milk made his bones strong, and as I said before, the candy gave me cavities. We both loved HipHop. We didn't have a lot of money to buy equipment, so we DJ'd on one record player. It was called a Dorchester.

He was just like me, but he spoke Spanish. We were inseparable. If he had a girlfriend, I'd date her friend. He had a sister and two brothers. They stayed with their mom. His dad didn't live with them.

Sometimes we would check my Dad on the corner, and get some money, then walk to the Bronx and see his Dad on a different corner and attempt to get money from his Dad too.

My Mother loved Frank. He is my best friend, and he loved her cooking.

Frank and I got jobs together, got fired together, quit together, and did graffiti together. He was Lord Jeze, and I was KNGAMPRCK as I said earlier.

We also made stupid decisions together. One day his cousin told us to fill out an application to work for New York City Transit Authority. We never filled that application out. We laughed and joked saying, "Nobody wants to be a train man." Twenty-five years later, we could've retired making double 300K a year or even more, but our adolescent minds couldn't see that logic.

I Don't Know Why
She Was Proud Of Me

When my Mother used to put me on punishment, Frank used to stay in the hallway, or I'd sneak him in my room and hide him in my closet. His mom didn't cook that much so I'd split with him my fried pork chops, sweet peas, and yellow rice she would make for dinner.

When she caught on to him being hidden in my closet, he had to stay out in the hallway and talk to me through the wall.

Frank grew tired of that routine, because I stayed on punishment too much, so he would go on his own adventures. I had to serve my time on punishment. Sometimes his mom would leave for a day or two, and his sister would have to take care of their lil bros Jacob and Russell.

Frank is the coolest dude of all. We looked up to each other, and I taught him how to read, with my Sesame Street and encyclopedia education. He felt school was *whack* to him the same as me.

The chicks dug him. He was light skinned, and the girls loved his brown hair. We both didn't get caught up in the high top fade or hair braided phase. We both got low cut Caesar's at the barber shop, and I was glad to be his pal. We struggled together, starved together, triumphed together, and did dirt together.

Frank and I actually formed a HipHop group as we were getting older. We linked up with some cats from the Bronx. They were going to the studio and had a group. I had a M.C. partner as well. His name was M.C.L. The

I Don't Know Why She Was proud Of Me

Great and we would rap together. Frank was our DJ but the routines we rehearsed were heavily influenced Run DMC.

Our Group wasn't prospering, and Frank went into production, so he had to be replaced by another DJ by the name of Wiz Rob from the Polo Grounds. We got a chance to perform in front of Dr. Bob Lee, a famous radio personality in New York City, and The Legendary Devastating Tito from the Fearless Four.

I had a promotional record on the radio that ran into the summer, and then this production company I signed with N.O.T Productions, released a single for me called "Check Me Out Baby." Throughout the year, I was buzzing compliments of the Kool DJ Red Alert. I also worked with the legendary DJ Masterdon. He made a classic HipHop record called Funkbox. He was mad cool and lived across the street from The Jumbo Spot.

I also was introduced to the now Legendary DJ Ron-G from the Polo Grounds. Back then, he was the youngest in charge. He'd invite me up to his apartment in the Polo Grounds and we'd get busy making songs.

I had made contact with my sister Melinda. She was staying on Hamilton Place in Downtown Harlem with her family. I can recall seeing my sister once or maybe twice within a year, and then one day, I came to visit, and she disappeared. I was hurt and I needed to find my lil sister. I searched for decades with no luck.

I Don't Know Why
She Was Proud Of Me

The crack era swept through neighborhoods and destroyed families. It even got inside the Junior High School. I saw my assistant gym teacher coming out the crack spot.

He was a white man, and he was a basehead. His father had owned a store across the street from the school. I could tell he looked and seemed different while at the gym, and he was absent from class a lot too. When I saw him coming from the sketchy looking building, I kind of figured things out.

I was really into girls now I was having sex. The crack wave caught one of my light skinned green eyed cuties. She was on it heavy, like overnight.

My friends and I were running, laughing, and joking one day and one of my friend's man said come to my house. I want to show y'all something. It was Porn a Vanessa del Rio Joint and Bad Mamma Jamma.

Bad Mamma Jamma was a big woman serving dudes with that *Good Good*. This was my first time being exposed to porn on VHS. Dudes were like let me hold that b…. He was like "How? You Lil ngz don't even have a VCR and y'all moms wouldn't even let you watch this."

We were young, dumb, broke, and possibly hungry. I had just gotten off of punishment. I wanted to continue pursuing my career in HipHop. I was always writing and listening to the radio. I had a Sharp gf 777 boombox; it was beat up. But it worked. I think I found it in the trash, which was my first studio. That's where I listened to

I Don't Know Why
She Was proud Of Me

Teddy Ted, Special K, The Awesome Two, and The World-Famous Mr. Magic Rap Attack Show and 92 KTU. That Sharp gf 777 allowed me to hook up a mic to it and you could over dub and make instrumentals until forever. The Boombox had an echo chamber on it too.

I had to follow up what I did with DJ Ron-G, the youngest in charge at the time. I had gained some popularity. I was buzzing in my neighborhood. So much that Wip Wop a young hustler from Esplanade Gardens cosigned me. I even got a spot on the Gangster group from Harlem Mobstyle's second album called "Game of Death." I was on the song called "Rolling 10 Deep." I had a small crew. We all met in junior high school. Some went to jail. Some died, and some are lucky to be alive today.

When we smoked our first blunt, we were hooked right then and there. We drank our first 40 ounce of Olde English malt liquor, we were drunk and high as ever. We were walking in and out of oncoming traffic laughing uncontrollably, out our minds.

We needed to know where'd he got that weed from. The malt liquor was easy to get; it cost $2.00 from the liquor store. But when you're young and broke that was hard to come by sometimes. Some of us would depend on someone in the family be it a mother, sister, uncle, or somebody or just hustle up so we'd have $5.00 or so to chip in for the stuff.

Some folks smoked Branson weed. We had some less expensive weed, it was called Hermans. One day we were cutting school again. This time we were anxious because we knew or hoped our man would come with the weed so we could smoke again. We liked smoking weed and how it made us feel. This was The chocolate strand, Buddha, cest, skunk, and Hawaiian.

We preferred rolling up White Owl cigars or Phillies versus folks who smoked in Bambu. It made us feel like every day was sunny. You could do anything and everything was beautiful. It made the element of danger where we lived more intense.

As a teenager, you do stupid things for no good reason. But Frank took no part in drinking and smoking. I once let Frank have some of my 40 ounce and he got very violent, it was difficult to hold him down. He could've killed someone. I never gave him any of my beer again.

Overall life was good, with the weed or without the weed, but with the weed it made everything look like viewing Harlem in 8K. We were kids, barely 14 and 15.

My friend was listening to his Walkman, but this wasn't the ordinary Walkman. This was a Sony Boodu Khan with matching headphones. The set was about $500.00 and when he put those headphones on my head, I heard that max bass and the comfort of the headphones on my ears. I was hooked on the sonics that real raw Harlem sound produced By Teddy Riley and Doug E. Fresh. I had never heard sonics clearly from music like that ever. It was the ultimate analog experience.

I Don't Know Why
She Was proud Of Me

Then he played NWA "Straight out of Compton." Imagine being a child, hearing that west coast boom bap for the first time. Mind you no one in rap or music period ever spoke or rapped with such force and rage like that before period.

We were getting high smoking on Skunk and Buddha and listening to the latest music by The real NGZ N.W.A with the best quality headphones on the market. While being in awe and high out of our minds taking turns with the headphones and being incredibly careful not to break them, I noticed dude. He started talking to my man on the side because that was his lil man.

We knew dude but they were from the same block, they grew up together. He was explaining to him what crack was and how to sell it. I started ear hustling again. I was the nosiest of all. "I want to get paid too." I said it and I meant it.

I was tired of scraping up to drink 40's and not having leather jackets and dope boots, hats, and sneakers. This dude had it all new spot bilt high tops, forty below Timberlands. He actually had three pairs of those: Avirex, Pelle Pelle, and AJ acid washed jeans with the leather trim, and Tale Lord jeans. This dude even had Eddie Bauer interior in his car, but he was like you *ain't* ready for this.

He was a Lieutenant. He'd distribute the work amongst the Pitchers, which is the name we used for the drug sellers back then. I guess he didn't think I was mature

I Don't Know Why She Was Proud Of Me

or smart enough, whatever. But he took all of us to the SPOT anyway.

It was an abandoned apartment. It was like the first day on the job. The kitchen had eight pies stacked on top of one another. That was that hardened. It hadn't been scraped and bottled yet and I didn't know. What the fuck I was doing. All I know is I was in a SPOT high out my mind laughing and joking with my friends. We all were high, playing with the crackheads. Smashing their fingers in the peephole when they reached for their Jumbo.

The Pitchers that were working the SPOT were clicking. Dude was selling two for 5ives, and I think treys which were slightly bigger. We were so dumb we didn't know it was illegal, we didn't care. We we're just on the job Lil ngz learning and fucking up shhht. But the bosses and lieutenants weren't playing. They understood this was not no game.

"Y'all lil ngz keep playing," one of the Lieutenants said. This was about money, and you could do football numbers in jail over this stuff if you get caught. With that being said, some dudes actually got the shit smacked out of them. Some got hands and feet put on 'em. And even Pistol whipped and forced to walk down the block naked. Especially, If you came up short, even my dumb young ass knew that.

My crew never got pressed like that. We we're the Power Posse and at this point I was KNGAMPRCK. I took dudes girls. I bagged girls, and if you tried to front

I Don't Know Why She Was proud Of Me

and talk to my girl one of my dudes would brass knuckle that jaw straight like that.

We were dangerous and could be deadly at times. Knucklehead lil dudes. We were out of our minds. I remember my Mom had to get my Dad to talk to me because the streets had me. I always considered my Mother's wellbeing, her emotions, and her bills. I told her I had a job. She didn't know I was cutting school to be in the streets. She wondered where all this money was coming from, and what job pays this much.

I often would have conversations with her about my day. She would ask me how was your day, and I would describe it vividly, lying like I've done in the past about school. Then she would ask me how was my music coming along, and I would tell her it was going just fine. We were trying to get signed to a record label and she would say, "Okay." She had no clue as to what I was really up to, day in and day out.

She gazed at me with admiration. Her eyes were saying look at my beautiful boy all grown up now. We would dine on fish and chips from 145th Street on St Nicholas Avenue. Enjoying the seconds we had together because the blessing is in a second.

The money was flowing, and I didn't give a fuck. It was time for me to graduate from middle school into high school. She couldn't believe it. I did it. Everything I learned from watching hours of Sesame Street and 3 2 1 Contact and School House Rock paid off.

I Don't Know Why
She Was Proud Of Me

I was quite popular in high school. I would hear my music every day for a year on the Kool DJ Red Alert 5:00 o'clock free ride radio show. He and Wendy Williams were on the air together on 98.7 Kiss FM New York.

She liked my song, "Check Me Out Baby" and gave me a what would be today the equivalent of a like. In these times, being broadcasted over the Tristate area live on the radio was huge.

One day my Dad sat me down and said, "Billy you selling drugs?"

I said, "No."

But folks already told him they saw me. They described me. Thoughts running through my mind, *someone snitched on me*. We'll keep that person's ID unknown for now.

I thought I had a high paying job. I worked an 8:00 PM to 8:00 AM shift, so at 8:00 AM, I had finished my shift and that was the time to wake up to go to school. I wasn't feeling that after a hard night of serving fiends. So, the times dudes were going to the clubs and flossing throughout the night, I was perched up high and could see everything in the courtyard of the SPOT. Similar to Nino in the corridor or exactly like that.

I could also hear when the lookout would yell Five-O, which meant the cops were coming. I had a 500 pack of Jumbo's, four dime clips of powder in a glass bottle, and that shhht was moving. We had lines like your favorite coffee shop. We were quick with the customer service like your favorite chicken spot.

I couldn't finish high school, and hustle at the same time. I was a smart dumb nga, so I dropped out. I had to get a GED. I was making more than teachers and children's fathers.

She suspected something was wrong with me because I dropped out of high school. She told me to go find my Father, she needed to speak to him about me. So, I went around the corner and got him. Along the way, I was nervous, because I had lied to both of my parents about me selling drugs. When she found out, I dropped out of school, she was livid, and my Dad didn't take the news about it lightly either. I know he wanted better for me. I was on the same path he was on which only leads to jail or dead.

My Dad was like, "Do you know what could happen if you go to jail?"

I told my Dad, "I was *gonna* be chilling with him and we were *gonna* run shhht in jail."

My Dad had served at least ten years or more in one prison and about five in another. When he heard me say that he smacked FIRE out of me right in front of her. Mother was saddened by my stupidity and surprised at Father's reaction.

He told me, "I better never hear you say no stupid shhht like that again. You ain't built and ready for jail with

I Don't Know Why
She Was Proud Of Me

your stupid young ass. "We're not *gonna* be together in jail. It don't work like that." Then he left.

After speaking to Mom, I felt stupid. I figured out that even though Dad and Mom weren't together, she could call on him to straighten me out if need be.

Dad was probably embarrassed by my level of understanding of choices and consequences. But really, he should've blamed himself for leaving an impression on me that the only way we could have a stronger bond was being in jail with him. Where he'd been for half of his life at the time.

I still didn't give a fuck. Mom always told me what she says to me goes in one ear and comes out the other and it did. I took the slap like a champ. He bruised my face with it too, swole my shhht up. Dudes thought I got snuffed, I told them what happened. I still went outside and sold my drugs on the same block my Dad lived on. It was nothing he could do or anyone for that matter. I was fully out of control, and I needed more than prayer.

"I don't know why she was proud of me."

I'd see my Father coming and going through the hood like he wasn't my Dad just some nga in the street. He'd be in the barber shop getting a haircut, and I'd give him the what up nga nod, like he was my homie, total disrespect.

I knew our relationship was ill when we started selling Jumbos together. Not at the same time but for the same person. That was it for him. He stopped hustling.

I Don't Know Why She Was proud Of Me

I called a limo and went to one of my shorties' house uptown and sparked a blunt. I was in Harlem, and I was wild.

I'd smoke in the movie theater on 125th Street with my team. It could be people sitting in front of me. I'd kick my feet up on the chair next to them and blow smoke on the back of their heads and watch them cough.

The movie theatre attendant knew better to say anything. That Herman's weed would do it to yah. I had no feelings and fuck yours too. I had another aka it was The Brown Skinned Satan, and this was a version of me on Demon time.

The next time, I went to the movie theatre, it was closed; rumor has it someone got murdered and it would get shut down forever. But I thought about all the wrong I've done since I first tried weed in junior high. I was uncontrollably dope and no one could tell me nothing.

One morning, I was at the diner ordering some pancakes, cheese eggs, beef sausage, and orange juice for myself. I ate my food and left my $10 tip and stepped off. It was a warm rainy day then I went around the corner to see what's up with my man at the other SPOT.

I had about $400 on me, maybe $100 in singles and a small hundred pack. So, my pockets were bulging a bit when I left my man's SPOT. I was pulled up on by four white men in jeans black hoodies and hats turned backwards. And of course, they had their badges around their necks.

I Don't Know Why
She Was Proud Of Me

They grabbed me and asked where I was coming from. I said I was just taking a walk. They checked my pockets and found the $400 and a small 100 pack of black top capsules. They took my beeper, it started to vibrate, and they threw it in a puddle of water and said, "Look it's swimming." They forced me to look at it, I was mad. They handcuffed me and fucked me up in the backseat. Then they took me into the Dirty 30 precinct.

In the Dirty 30 they handcuffed me to a bench and called my Mother. Because I was a minor, they gave me a slap on the wrist. She was furious. Mom told me see what your ass get. The next time I'm not coming to get you.

But of course, everything she said went in one ear and came out the other. The cops was rolling up on dudes more frequently now in Harlem and we all felt it.

Some dudes got caught selling drugs and went to Rikers Island. Some went to group homes, and some went to Spofford. I continued to run in the streets.

I was very immature and the pressure from the cops got more intense. They would roll up in the SPOT with TNT (Tactical Narcotics Team) sometimes. They would have agents disguised as crackheads. We could tell the difference and refused sales. They just didn't look authentic. Those who couldn't tell, would end up in handcuffs. This was the crack wave within a crime wave, and a New York state of mind was Harlem all day.

I was still trying to hide the fact that I was still in those streets. This was before I had my first daughter Alysha. If

I Don't Know Why
She Was proud Of Me

Mother knew the jest of everything I was doing at this point, I doubt if she was proud of me.

Meanwhile, Frank moved to the Bronx. He had a new crew too and I was like, "I want to get money with y'all over there." It's too hot over here, but this hustle was different. It was all about guns and cocaine. I was a full-fledged goon at this time. I carried a Mac 10 inside my leather black and white Phat Farm messenger bag. Sometimes a 357 magnum on my waistline.

When I said Frank and I did everything together too, I mean everything. One time we went to the movies to see Tango and Cash. Sylvester Stallone and Kurt Russell starred in it. They were detectives and carried the exact same guns. Frank and I had on us right in the movie theatre. On the grand concourse in the Bronx.

Mother knew I was bad but not on this level. I was wilding in the Bronx taking dudes girls. No sympathy for *wack* players was my motto and I stood by it. I lived it.

My Mother was really focused. By this time, she had stable employment. I was fortunate to have seen her work a full-time job and flourish throughout a career with the NYPD. It was a longtime coming for her. She had gotten tired of all the shenanigans. The welfare center put people through a lot for that little money. She overcame what many women couldn't. She did more than just survive. She survived the ghetto.

I Don't Know Why She Was Proud Of Me

The mental and physical abuse she overcame, financial strife, and she did it all with a ladylike flair pocketbook and all.

Her hair looked stunning, healthy, and especially with a wash and roller set as always. It was long, black, and shiny. She would sometime wear it curled or have it in a straight ponytail. Always showing up on time whether at work or visiting friends.

I was happy for my Mother, and I celebrated her every day, especially on Mother's Day. Since I was a child making birthday cards for her, I bought her unique items that vendors would sell throughout the city, like paintings and handmade items. She placed them in her living room for company to gaze at.

She loved to watch DVDs, so I would buy her the latest movies and most of her favorites. I bought her a box set of 007 movies. She loved James Bond 007.

I once bought her a ticket to see Luther Vandross live. That was his last concert he'd perform at Radio Music Hall, before he produced "Dance With His Father." She had an exciting time.

I was trying to be a good son to her. My Mother enjoyed life, she had friends, coworkers, and her brother Gerald. He was the one who my Mother contacted when I told her I may have gotten someone pregnant. He was the one who questioned me over the phone.

He asked, "Did you have sex with her?"

I Don't Know Why
She Was Proud Of Me

"Yes."

"Did you use a condom?"

"No."

"Well then it could be yours."

After I answered the questions, that was that. I was happy and astonished at the same time. This was the first time I had found out what the use of condoms were for, and I found out the difference between liking it raw over using protection.

My Dad never had the talk with me about girls or the birds and the bees, or what to do when reaching that level of maturity. I was just going with the flow of things some call it the little head controlling the big head.

I loved Uncle Gerald. He had a home in Queens, a wife, and a child named Kanika. He was my role model. He had become a computer engineer at Polygram Records. When I came to his home, I used to see computer reels throughout his house to store data. Those were the equivalent to flash drives now.

He had a Technics amplifier and a mixer, and a pair of Panasonic Thrusters. I liked to take the covers off of them and see the woofers tremble. When the bass kicked, you could feel it inside your body.

My thing was the equipment, mostly the big knob on the amplifier which turned the sound up. The Gemini mixer with the 5 band eg. He wasn't about DJing, so he

I Don't Know Why She Was Proud Of Me

only had one turntable. He listened leisurely and professionally. He also had a sixteen band equalizer and a dual TEAC cassette tape machine.

The led meters used to fascinate me as I watched the strip lights monitor the music. The buttons and knobs intrigued me and triggered my HipHop soul.

I would readjust my Uncle's settings on the machines, and I would get yelled at. My ears wasn't mature enough for enhancing sound or at least that's what my Uncle thought. I was so compelled to touch the switches and push the buttons in and out. I'd click some switches on and off. Slide the faders and look at the red and black cords on the back of the equipment.

He also had a beta max and a video disc player. This was a new machine used to view movies in your home that came in a format that was larger than a full length album. You'd have to slide it in the machine and pull down the lever.

Kanika and I would feel vibrations of the energy coming from my Uncle's basement parties in Queens, from the floor. We could hear the music flowing through the staircase. He had all of the classic R&B and soul albums and he was groovy.

Mom and my Uncle were the best of friends outside of the other friends that partied with them on the weekends. My Aunt Serena didn't like the basement parties in her home. My Mother partied with the basement crew heavy.

I Don't Know Why
She Was proud Of Me

My Uncle used to make a mean lasagna, and chopped barbecue where he used a special hatchet. My Aunt stayed in her room with the door closed or went to see her family.

Once the basement party was over, in the morning, I'd go downstairs and go through my Uncle's stuff. I'd bypass the bottles of beer, liquor, cigarette butts and roaches in the ashtray. I'd head straight to the equipment. I loved it, and the way it sounded.

Later on, in life my Mother and her sister-in-law would grow close. The party people in the basement would all pass away years later. First Leslie, Grandma, then Grandpa, Uncle Gerald, then Aunt Mimi, Aunt Serena, Mother, and then Cousin Tony.

I met the Mother of my first two children Kim. Alysha and Lisa are our daughters. I asked God to bless me with two little girls. One beautiful and the other one just as beautiful. But the oldest was to take care of the younger one, like a good big sister and she does that till this day.

We raised our kids to be college graduates. They have thriving careers as healthcare professionals. One is head nurse in Bellevue Medical Center, and the other is a traveling nurse.

But back to me and Frank. He had his new crew, and we were Deep. We were the True Villain. We all got tatted, and we were getting money. I was still smoking and drinking and wilding. As I said before, Frank never smoked nor did drugs and only drank once when he got

I Don't Know Why
She Was Proud Of Me

violent. But me, I'd be listening to NWA all the time. I had that mentality.

Meanwhile, my Mother had no idea of the full extent of my thuggery and criminal activities that were going on. She probably thought, I was just chillin' with Frank like he had chilled at my house when we were younger. I was actually living with him.

One day, I was in the Bronx pitching snow. On the block, I forget which one; but if you know the X, it's up that long ass staircase in the middle of the block. I had just finished my shift, and I was replaced by my man Chris.

I went to chill with Kim, and I was on my way to take her back to Harlem with me. Frank and Floyd approached me with tears almost forming in their eyes. They said Chris had just gotten murdered he was shot in the head at point blank range. I was mad, sad, enraged and fueled with anger. I was ready to get the guns and get to it, but they told me fall back. It was handled like I knew it would be.

The murder of Chris really stunned me. I felt death knocking at my door back then. The Bronx was way iller than Harlem and I had to lay low. So, I went back home and stayed with my Mom for a while.

She had changed into a brand new woman and still lived on 145th Street. She was content and had met a new man. His name was Richard. He would become her husband, and I would be their witness at a City Hall wedding. Later, she would regret staying married to him for almost 13 years.

I Don't Know Why
She Was proud Of Me

I was back in Harlem now still being stupid. I had a youthful offender charge, and I was still in the streets. I was charged with possession of a controlled substance with intent to distribute.

Hustling in a residential building, I guess the neighbors didn't appreciate my presence and the traffic. I was doing my thing again and someone called 911 on me. I was hard at work making my sales, and then the police rushed into the building. They arrested the look out.

I tried to run but I fell up the stairs, and eventually got handcuffed again and sentenced with five years' probation. With no trip to Rikers Island, which spared me the agony of channeling my inner savage.

I don't know why she was proud of me. I couldn't even be a crime boss. I was a pitcher, a soldier, a thug, who was fortunate to live long enough to realize any level of criminal activity is nothing to be proud of.

What I did gain as a kid living this lifestyle was the experience of being in the streets of Harlem.

Kim was hood as hell and so was I. We'd drink 40 ounces; smoke blunts and play the "Above the Rim" soundtrack over and over again. And of course, Mary J. Blige's "What's the 411" remix album.

My cousin Kanika came to live with us at this time. I had to stop hustling because I wanted to be around to raise my kids. I didn't want to take any more chances,

I Don't Know Why She Was Proud Of Me

risking my freedom. That was a particularly crucial decision for me.

Fatherhood was something that I took extremely seriously. I felt a natural sense of responsibility and compassion. I wanted to be there every step of the way. It was an important thing to be the first one to see your baby walk.

It was a joy to build the cribs and put the bumpers on. Sterilizing bottles, buying Pampers® never the other knock off brands like Fitti, which made your babies pampers sag in the back. We had our King Vitamin and Kaboom Cereal moments, but they were brief. We had our first child Alysha, and we spoiled her as much as we could. When Kim got pregnant with our second daughter Lisa, we did the same with her as well. The struggle was beautiful.

David Dinkins was a good Mayor. He was inspirational. He was our 106th Mayor of New York City. He was the first African American Mayor of New York City. A great tennis player, and he was an author.

Through his administration, he helped a lot of poor people get through the housing system quickly. We had a Section 8 voucher which allowed us to live in a nice, renovated apartment anywhere in NYC paying extraordinarily little in rent.

Unfortunately, at this time, my Dad had died from HIV. He died in the month of October 1993. My daughter

I Don't Know Why
She Was proud Of Me

was born in November 1993. He was survived by me and his two daughters Melinda and Nefertiti.

I would go to see him after my various little jobs I held. One evening after work, I came to visit him at Harlem Hospital and his room was empty. One of the nurses on the floor had told me he died. I was sad, and I felt sort of lost and incomplete.

He wasn't able to see any of his six grandkids. He was my Dad, and I did love him. As far as being a better Father towards us, I think he could've done better for me and my sisters while he was here.

Never forget little Black girls need a responsible father that's *gonna* be fair, caring, with understanding, and a sense of strength and be gentle with her feelings. Being street smart and not family oriented, stole this up bringing from my sisters.

Sons need stability to mirror off, everything masculine the father has to offer. Positively strategically flawed male to reflect upon that was my Dad; now that I'm successful in raising my own children from babies to adults. I've been creating a positive impact on their lives. I see what a devoted father is like with kids out of wedlock.

R.I.P. Billy Lip. I'm sorry and I love you. He did what he did, and I got to spend some time with him. I can recall him taking my sister Melinda and I to Yankee Stadium when we were younger. My sister Melinda remembers it more vividly than I do. I guess that was his attempt to create a bond between us.

I Don't Know Why
She Was Proud Of Me

My Father had gone to rest. I was a dad. I had a family now. Kim and I were deep in the beautiful struggle, but we were young, and I was a smart dumb nga. I would often wonder why my Mother was proud of me.

I was reckless throughout my childhood and into my early adulthood twenties. I had measured my sexual appetites stamina against pornographic videos. I was a lover of aunties, sisters, mothers, and wives. I was a cheater, a womanizer, and I kept my pimp hand strong. I was a goon, an enforcer, and an ill brother. I was terrible. I had the streets as a role model, and my focus on school and positivity was off.

I had shaved off my hair and was on some onyx shhht. Yes! The rap group. I had an NWA attitude one hundred miles and running. I'd walk eight miles a day enjoying the New York experience. I'd ride on public transportation to The Staten Island Ferry and took a chick with me for an adventure. I had a reputation.

My mindset was of a brown skinned lunatic. And I may have burned some bridges with some folks. I was smoking Hawaiian, but I hadn't gotten into smoking cigarettes yet. I thought cigarettes was yucky and they made people's breath stink. They really did. But not my Mother's breath. She kept a pack of big red chewing gum on deck, and now I know why. Once I did start smoking cigarettes, I know my breath stunk too.

I was loyal to my Crew True Villain and my children. I would never let my kids down. We bought them Harry

I Don't Know Why She Was proud Of Me

Potter books to read. Kept them in the beauty Parlor. Wearing fresh leathers, Michael Jordan sneakers. Guess outfits from Cookies, Nautica and custom made jackets from boutiques on Broadway. Some grown women felt a certain way of how they were pampered and rocked the same hairstyles as them.

The reason why I asked God for daughters, so they could have someone to play with and create a strong sibling bond with one another. That's something I never had.

I got lonely as a child, but I dealt with it. I would not let my children have a hint of what I was exposed to growing up. Kim kept their braids tight. She would do styles that had my daughters' names braided with their natural hair. She is a great mother and nurturer. She had even taken on the responsibility of raising her little brother Vince, while her mom did a jail bid. She put up with all my bullshit, until she couldn't take it no more.

Kim trusted me with her everything. But I cheated on her, and we broke up. My Mother loved her. And we still remain great friends till this day, despite the stuff we went through in our twenties.

One sunny afternoon, she threw my clothes and CDs out of the bedroom window when she found girls' phone numbers. I tried to hide them in my sneakers, so I quickly picked my clothes up off the sidewalk and placed them in the trunk of Frank's Lexus GS 300. And went to live with him for a while in Castlehill Projects in upper Bronx New York.

Frank was in the streets heavy, and so was the rest of the crew. We had some OGs, me, Frank, and David. We would be the youngins in the crew. I was still rapping and pursuing a career in HipHop, and they felt my passion.

I loved David as well, who was awfully close to me and Frank. He was a great guy. He was a dark skinned dude, who had all the ladies. He drove a Pearl White Lexus 450. He'd pick me up and run me around the town flossing on suckers without trying, so I thought.

He'd take me to pick up my kids and bring them home just like Frank would. We called him Prince D. David who had a connection with a guy who was in the music industry. He had a small record label. I can't remember his name. But he gave David a position as president of a subsidiary label under his record label.

David signed me to True Villain Records. He had a beautiful family. A nice mother and I believe he had three brothers, a sister, and a daughter at the time. He was an angel Rest In Peace D.

He was killed by a stray bullet on a sweltering summer day in Crotona Park in the Bronx. His family witnessed it. That was a sad time in our lives and for his family. He was a good dude. They don't make them like that anymore.

Meanwhile, my Mother was progressing with her new job working for the city. She had come a long way. She

I Don't Know Why She Was Proud Of Me

was cleaning parks at one time and that wore her down. Imagine a diva hard on her luck cleaning parks, lifting garbage bags, and cleaning bathrooms. She had risen like a phoenix from those types of jobs and now she was working outside the chief of patrol of NYPD office.

I had to really chill now because I've been in so much trouble already. I couldn't mess that up for her. So, I got jobs here and there with Frank of course. He and I had gotten jobs working at the movie theatre in Coop City in the Bronx. I was still living with them while his family expanded.

Once he met his wife Tasha, a Brooklyn girl with a strong family background and goddess like qualities, they had a son and a daughter Frank Jr and Taylor. I was happy for them.

Frank was still a True Villain. Moving and shaking with the best of them. He hadn't completely left the game. He was in nightclubs pulling up in his 850 BMW like nga this is us. As the song "NO Scrubs" by the girls TLC played on New York's Hot 97, I was on the passenger side in my man's ride hollering at chicks too. I bagged a couple and broke some more hearts. You know how young ngz do.

Although I had a room in his crib, I kind of was still living with my Mother too. She was in Harlem with her Husband. I would come by and visit her. I still had keys to the apartment and had my room there. I was still man

I Don't Know Why
She Was Proud Of Me

of her house because Richard her husband was not a good man to her.

He was a strong man with a heroin addiction. He was also a United States Veteran. He had children too, a daughter and a son. I don't believe he was regularly active in their lives either.

His Buddies, called him Indian because of his hair. I once punched him in the face over some jelly in the refrigerator. I was the nightmare of dealing with a woman that has a young thug for a son.

Back to the life outside, Frank and I would go to the studio and lay some tracks down. Pee Wee Kirkland the Basketball legend became our manager, and we made some demos with Stik E and the Hoods. They're famous for the song "Shake What Your Mamma Gave Ya!"

We hadn't made it big on the music scene yet, but I do remember The Notorious B.I.G saying in one of his songs, "Don't be mad UPS is Hiring." Biggie Smalls was the illest rapper in the world. He once stood in front of FYE, a music store that used to be on 52nd Street in Midtown Manhattan. He listened to me rhyme one time. R.I.P. Christopher "Notorious B.I.G" Wallace. So, I got myself a parttime job at UPS as a pre-loader and worked there for ten years.

During my time there, I had many situations I put myself in. One of them was my hours. My shift started at 3:15 am. This was at the time that the infamous Tunnel Night Club was poppin on Sundays, So I couldn't attend

I Don't Know Why She Was Proud Of Me

any of those special iconic performances and thrilling times real HipHopers from all over the world lived through in the heart of New York City.

Second, I was going through some personal issues with my HipHop, Fatherhood, and Quality of life as well which caused me to drink and smoke more frequently. I called these moments, 'My by Myself Parties'.

One day I couldn't keep up with the rapid pace of the boxes coming down the conveyor belt. I just said fuck it and passed out in one of the trucks while the boxes piled up at the end of the line.

My supervisor, who was also named William, lived in the Polo Grounds up in Harlem. He caught my slacking and went in the truck I was in. He looked down at me shaking his head laughing. I was finished, bent, and high off of weed and liquor.

He was built like Dolph Lundgren from Rocky IV, and he was studying to be a Doctor. I once used my benefits to see a mental therapist because I was so depressed about my love life and music career. I'd often get back massages too. This relieved my tense muscles due to the grueling work I had to do at UPS. The benefits were great, but then I made a grave mistake of crossing over to the management side of things. During that time, the workers' union went on strike.

There was a huge blown up rat outside of the entrance of the building and a picket line. You could seriously get hurt by crossing the picket line or if you were on the other side of the infamous Teamsters union, which was corporate, and I was the supervisor. Ultimately, after ten years, I had to depart.

I also had a part time job at a printing shop, and I moved back to my Mother's crib temporarily. Our single didn't take off it was entitled, "You Are What I'm All About."

I had to help feed my family. Kim and I had a system to where I get the kids any time I wanted. So, I got them every weekend, summertime, holidays, and we split birthdays. This allowed my Mother to spend time with her Grandkids celebrating all the holidays and graduations.

When I attended birthday parties Kim's new man was present too. We were cool and respectful. No problems amongst the men. You can say we were blessed moving forward.

I had a job, and I was living with my Mother, and I was helping her with her rent, bills, etc. One of Frank's friends, who was also a friend of mine, saw I was struggling. He knew me to be responsible due to my fatherhood and co-signs from Frank. He hooked me up with a gig as a security guard working at a studio called The Hit Factory.

This was a time when I would see Wyclef Jean, Jimmy Cozier, and I even had a spat with the late great Luther Vandross. At this time, I had witnessed a lot of things in my short lifespan thus far.

I Don't Know Why
She Was Proud Of Me

I've witnessed my babies come out of their mother's womb. I've seen the saying what goes around comes around happen before my eyes. I was about to witness another one of my babies enter into this world.

It was a cold and cheery holiday season. It was me, my Aunt Muriel and Stephanie's mother Amanda. Stephanie is the mother of my third daughter. My baby girl Ashley Magnifisense.

I was walking back and forth from our apartment on 145th Street to Harlem Hospital on 135th Street anticipating the birth of our Christmas baby.... It was on Christmas Eve that we were blessed with a baby girl Ashley Patricia Magnifisense Brown. She shares the name of my Mother Patricia. Her sister's named her Ashley. I had a lot of baby cribs in her apartment and tough times did hit.

I had known what it was like to get food stamps. I had known what it was like to reach out to folks in the street and ask for help. I also took on a job at the airport. It was mostly a curiosity thing.

A generous Azie Faison from Mobstyle used to hit me off with a few dollars here and there. Some might know of him being portrayed as Ace in the film "Paid in Full."

When I needed something, I'd call him, and he'd tell me to meet him at the location 132. I'd be very patient because I knew he was a busy individual, but he'd come through.

I Don't Know Why
She Was Proud Of Me

I had known what it was like having filled out that long colorful form. Waiting for my benefits card to come in the mail. I didn't receive emergency food stamps. It sucked and that phase of being on public assistance didn't last too long.

I continued to seek employment and my Mother was incredibly supportive of me and my ever growing family. I had been through a lot at this point. I felt blessed to reach the point where I needed to set a positive example for my children. So, I took them to several parks, and we went to different children's functions throughout the city.

I took them to libraries and bought them books and tried to encourage them to read. I also traveled down to Maryland with them to visit my Uncle Gerald and Aunt Serena frequently. They had moved from Queens Village and had a house in Prince George's County in Maryland. We had some of the most memorable times.

All the cousins were together my Aunties, and of course my Mommy. She loved her Aunt Muriel. She was her favorite relative aside from my Uncle Gerald.

We all would sing and dance to Earth Wind and Fire songs. My Uncle was a great air guitarist. The children, including me, would watch him play while running around laughing and dancing.

Here is my life at the time as a so called Christian. My Mother's stepmom was a deaconess in a church right around the corner from us in Harlem. I'd take my daughters there, so that they could have a relationship with her as well.

They attended that church regularly on Sundays and went to Sunday School there too. I wanted them to know Jesus and I wanted to restructure my mind, body, soul, and spirit. I became a Christ seeker, and I found Jesus. He was within me. I brought my children along. My Mommy sometimes too. Because I loved my Grandmother, and I wanted my Mother and her family to be cool. She called her Ms. Vi.

I hadn't surrendered totally to Christ though. I would still smoke weed and drink after the service with my new crew that consisted of Stephanie's sisters and people from the building.

We would go $2.50 plus $2.50 on a bag of Buddha. Frank and Tasha used to commend me on my efforts to be a better person and tell me my musical efforts would one day pay off.

She admired my musical efforts, and she had been watching me since birth go through various phases in life. Now, I was a father of three girls trying to set a prime example better than any man she had been with including her dad.

I had met this cool cat at a job I worked at in Times Square. His name was Arthur Rutledge. He was another guy my Mom and I admired and loved. He also admired and loved us. We shared the same love for HipHop,

I Don't Know Why
She Was Proud Of Me

movies, and just life in general from a Harlem perspective.

When he met her, he immediately loved her cooking, especially her chili. He even ate the bay leaves she used to add flavor. He called her Big Momma, and he was very respectful and charming to all the ladies. On Valentines Day, he'd buy all the legal aid assistants roses. He used to say her cooking was second to his Grandmother's.

I introduced him to my daughters back then as well. They enjoyed his company and found him to be the life of any party. He saw my treks and movements as a Baby Daddy riding trains up and down the city getting my kids and returning them to their mothers safely.

I was trying to inspire him if he ever encountered a situation such as mines to be responsible at all costs. He was intelligent and clever he already knew that. I had toned my behavior down somewhat, especially around my children. I don't think they ever saw me smoke or even cuss around them.

Arthur was unique and savvy with his style of dress. He was from Harlem, the Eastside Projects on 103rd Street. He would show love to everyone he encountered. He was maybe three years younger than me, but he had an old soul.

I had been working at a law firm in midtown Manhattan for some time now. He and I would go to work throughout the week, and on the weekends, we would get together and party while listening to music. He was the

I Don't Know Why She Was proud Of Me

one who put me on to the rap group Heltah Skeltah, a Brooklyn rap duo.

He scared me once because I heard him throwing up in the bathroom. I asked, "Are you aight?" because he was really throwing up violently. I opened the door of the bathroom and I saw he was throwing up blood. He waved it off as nothing, but it looked serious to me.

We had lunch together regularly. Working with him every day made Corporate America a beautiful place to start a career in. He was critical of my rapping ability, and he wanted me to work harder.

Lunchtime came around one afternoon, I had to get some toys for my kids at The Times Square Toys-R-Us. On my way there, I met a young lady. She was light skinned and thick. She would become my love child accomplice bearing me sons within five years.

It would seem that what goes around had come around, and the cops would come to my job and serve me with a summons to appear in Family Court. One of my shorties had me served with papers for child support. Seventeen years later plus arrears. I was embarrassed, and Arthur thought it was mad funny, and it truly was, but it was unfortunate for me.

Some folks know about those child support payment blues, especially when you want to be in your child's life, but the mother makes it difficult.

I Don't Know Why
She Was Proud Of Me

One day this small Caucasian man came up to me like he was warning me, saying in a whispering tone "The cops are looking for you, you should make a run for it." This was New York and New Yorkers are different.

Eventually, I faced the cops, and they were there to serve me with the paperwork, to appear in court. They were used as an official escort for the young lady who was at a distance watching me get served. I watched the young lady walk away with the cops, switching her hips real hard. Her body language was saying see you in court nga.

This was a ploy to complicate my financial situation. A bitter baby mother. All of that was unnecessary. We could've talked it out, but she wanted to fight me in a different environment. Involving people who don't understand the makings of the Black family, or the frustrations that can occur within them.

You see she had papers on me like the "Richard "Dimples Fields" song I would often play on Yvonne Mobley after dark. I was petty and we lived in an environment where only the strong survived. Family comes first. With that being said, my Mother sided with me on all accounts even if it meant going along with a lie to get back at a girl who broke my heart. Whom I thought cheated on me.

I met a girl who was pregnant, and the child's father abandoned them. At first, I was unaware of the pregnancy. Eventually, I spoke to the father of her child. I mentioned to him that I would raise his son. The biological father was a goofy and he basically told me over the phone, "Fuck the girl and her baby." I said I'll raise the kid, because I wouldn't want any child to feel like nobody wanted to be a family with him, as I experienced as a child growing up.

My Mother was a protector and I never felt like I was without her well wishes. She was the glue in me and my children's lives. If the mother of my child allowed us time with each other, we maximized the family time when we could, using every second. Yes, she shared my frustrations and many disparities I experienced. She helped me stabilize the development of my fatherhood enough to co-parent once again.

Mom was my rock and pillar. She was a Pisces and a lonely widow. She was no push over. For all her life's experiences and encounters, she survived and here was another chapter.

I wonder why she was proud of me because of all I put her through. I was still chasing after God on repentance speed. She traveled to and from on the subway with me and my children. Whether they were in Yonkers, Harlem, Denver Colorado, or Brooklyn New York City. No Distance separated me from my children. I flew on planes, trains, automobiles, or walked. I was determined to make an impact on their lives and never wanted them to feel like my Dad made me feel.

Birthdays were special. We enjoyed our birthday cakes and songs. It would just be Mommy, me, and her grandkids. I was a Baby Daddy. Kim calls me that, I don't run from that title either, and she showed up at my 50th birthday party and my wife and I showed up at hers as well.

My Mom supported me and my love for children, whether biological, or non-biological. I have six children. I had them all by the age of thirty-eight. She contributed to their upbringing since conception and never once closed her door to the mothers of my children.

She provided food, shelter, monetary support, and cooking tips, advice to help the young women become better for their wellbeing of her son throughout the battles in court over my rights as a father. She had my back. It's just that New York City instinct called a New York state of mind. And through the grace of God, this was unveiled after all the shenanigans and stress levels I put my Mother through.

I moved to Brooklyn first to start my new family with my new born son and my girlfriend at the time. I had gotten played by this shorty. She had gotten a one bedroom apartment around the corner from us. She would assist as well.

I got emotional and was feeling depressed because my shortie was stepping out on me, so I'd down fifths of Bacardi Razz, along with Mommy reflecting on our lives, up to that point. This was our drink and I believe this was a time when I enjoyed smoking cigarettes too, but you know how these things go, what goes around comes around again. I grew tired of manipulating women and stirring up emotions creating a toxic environment especially with kids involved.

I wanted to settle down and I did. The first thing I did was go to the Brooklyn Tabernacle and repent to God for all the wrongs I've done. I praised and worshipped God with The Brooklyn Tabernacle Choir, and it's Pastor Jim Cymbala. I asked for forgiveness, and I even got baptized again.

My Mother was present and so was my then fiancé. This was a turning point for me and my Mom. I would take her to church and my children regularly. I was deep in the church. I even went on Tuesdays and Thursdays.

Arthur, Frank, and Tasha thought I would become a Pastor. I had given up smoking and drinking after committing my life to the Lord. I was sober for years at this point.

I would get my daughters on the weekends and have them go to a church that teenagers attended in Times Square. I was trying to change. I chose Christ as my Lord and Savior. I also met a cool dude from Flatbush Brooklyn named Leon on the bus coming from Coney Island, visiting my son. He was an older fella. I thought he'd be a cool fit for my Mom. She had been single for a while, but they never clicked

Leon had a great personality, and he was Brooklyn all day. He was not rowdy. He was respectful, resourceful, streetwise, and generous. He was in support of me changing my life around.

I Don't Know Why
She Was Proud Of Me

Arthur knew a lady that was cool with the both of us. Back in the day, we'd drink and smoke together. She knew my past, and she and I became remarkably close. I would tell her my tales of controlling women and running the streets. I felt comfortable around her. She was a female friend that I admired. She always wore heels and dressed nicely, and she was a Brooklyn girl all day.

I asked her if she knew anyone who would like to hook up with a dude like me. Although we were cool, she didn't trust me, especially with her cousin's heart. Whom I had my eyes on for some time.

She was unlike any woman I had ever dealt with. I just felt that way, and unknowingly my Mother would be the beneficiary of her warmth and care, and I would have a chance with a genuinely good woman.

She had an angel and was a blessing that came out of nowhere who took I-95 from Maryland to Flatbush Brooklyn where I resided with Mother. I had lived in Brooklyn for almost eight years now on Nostrand and Avenue D then New York Avenue and Newkirk Avenue.

Arthur thought that she was the one for me. He told me I think that you should settle down with this young lady. She's smart and a heavyweight. He'd call thick women stuffing as well. He was crazy but he was my dude.

With constant prayer, phone calls, and repentance for nearly three years, plus surrendering to the Lord, I finally was awarded a date with this woman. I was persistent and she still wasn't feeling me. I guess she tolerated me

I Don't Know Why
She Was proud Of Me

because of her cousin and possibly my friend Arthur's influence over her.

We finally went on a date and to the movies. We watched the movie 300. This woman played hard to get with the cold shoulder all night, but I was determined to win her over. I even invited her to one of my shows, I did, and she watched me rock the mic one night. I even added a new a/k/a to my KNGAMPRCK Moniker.

I renamed myself William Extra because I always knew it was a lil something extra about me compared to the other William's out there. I opened up about my love and thankfulness for our Creator's mercy, and I incorporated my love for Him in my lyrics. I was like a peacock showing its feathers to appeal to my mate. I was really a lion in sheep clothing. I say a lion because I devour everything and bring it back to my family. In this case, I would get this woman, and be her king, as my zodiac sign labels me a Leo.

I would be fair to her and let her live out her choice to be a happy wife, and in return, I would have a happy life. Yeah, only if she'd allow it. I was about to pounce on her and make her mines by the grace of God. Although I was saved, I still had the streets in me enough to not be a simp but leave a great masculine impression on her son.

Eurdise and I had fallen in love in The Brooklyn Botanical Gardens. We'd have long distance dates and watch Lifetime movies together over the phone. We'd talk every morning when I traveled from Brooklyn to get my daughter Ashley and take her to school by train. She admired my fatherhood as well, and she immediately became a great support to my Mother.

Once I took her to Prince George's County to meet my family, Uncle Gerald, Aunt Serena, and my Cousins on Thanksgiving. Then we went to meet up with her family for the remainder of the evening.

I was introduced to her Aunties. They looked so young, although they had me and Eurdise by some years. I mistook them for being nosey young teenagers, at first glance, but as the night went on and we got to know each other, I could see the womanhood and wisdom in all of them as we enjoyed one another's presence and fellowship during this holiday time.

They found me to be charming and a good soul to be around, and then I met with the matriarch of the family. She was really straightforward and told me to respect and treat her niece good or she was *gonna* get me.

Eudy said if you get approval from her, I would be cleared and adored in the family. I was accepted and we had a pleasant time. We all enjoyed ourselves, with a large table full of food, non-alcoholic drinks, desserts of all sorts from tarts to the sweet chocolate cream cake, and good positive vibes amongst these children of God.

I also met her son too. He was well mannered and a young teen, a sponge willing to soak up everything the world has to offer. If I were to be the male influence in his life, I would have to be direct, firm, easy and open with him coming from a strong male Black perspective. His name is Shakeem, and I would never have him be a witness to the horrors a stepfather could produce in the home as I've seen at first hand.

Eurdise's finger got a ring put on it because I loved her and always have. She was different from other ladies I've dealt with. She does not smoke, nor drink and she was from the hood like me. She graduated from Berkley College, and we had a chemistry of our own. I proposed to her in Washington DC's Botanical Gardens.

I also took on a job at the airport to better my income. It was mostly a curiosity thing since I was a child and I had one of those toy airports.

She was happy during this time enjoying her retirement. She figured that she'd done enough and had reached the level of prestige in her life, to walk away from her duties as a member of the NYPD. She grew comfortable in her new path of life as a retiree.

Mom loved her family, friends, relatives, and also life as she knew it. She loved going to the movies, especially seeing James Bond. This was the last movie we were able to take her to see. She was not athletic or the physical type. She was a girlie girl, and she loved dancing, singing, smiling, and wearing things that looked cute and pretty. I could see her in the kitchen right now making black eyed peas, white rice and smoked turkey necks singing Kenny Roger's hit song "Lady" intensely.

I Don't Know Why She Was Proud Of Me

She loved her long black hair and as she aged it turned grey. She would get rinses and then she just let it go, Full grey. Then, she went to the hair stylist and got locks.

When the spread of COVID became prevalent, we wore masks everywhere we went to supermarkets and shopping malls. She was pleased at her fresh look, and she took pleasure waking up and catching the shuttle to the senior center and being in their company. She formed many more special friendships. She would go to see plays, extraordinary events, the occasional casino runs with Ms. Joanne who, amidst my Mother's passing, she was her current Bestie. I still keep in touch with Ms. Joanne.

Mom and my wife got the news over the phone due to a routine checkup and blood work. Stage four ovarian cancer had been detected and was advised to move forward with aggressive chemo treatments.

My wife would race down the highway from Maryland to New York City in Brooklyn and then to my Mother's appointments in Queens, while I had out of town business to handle.

My Mother and I are extremely fortunate to have a woman such as my wife Eurdise in our lives. She is a Virgo, and she was my Mother's angel. She gave her a 70th birthday bash and we used Zoom so all of her friends far and near could attend. It was just us and the kids with her in person. She was very tired because she had a chemo session that day too; it was one of her first. From there her strength went up and down based on the cocktails they administered.

When She resided at home with us her room was next door to ours, on the same floor; but it became difficult for her to walk up our three story townhome stairs. It took much strength and balance to climb the stairs. She used to walk really fast up those stairs when she was at her optimum Patricia. Intravenously Patricia received nutrition and had to have blood transfusions once a week on top of chemo if necessary.

Often, I'd asked Mom "Are you *gonna* fight this thing Mommy?"

She would say, "I'm a try Billy...."

I said, "Okay Mommy...."

Next, we drove to her appointment. The chemotherapy sessions had brought me back to the times when my Mother and I would be at the welfare center. It was a totally different vibe, but the togetherness just reminded me of those times.

The facility was where people were fighting for their lives. The young and elderly were there dealing with their different forms of cancer. Nurses showing absolute compassion while administering treatments and drawing blood.

Some folks were upbeat with family members beside them, and some were there with no one. The music they played was classic soul. We'd enjoyed the playlist and the busy environment. Sometimes we'd stay for five hours. The medicine would knock her out.

I'd sometimes take my Ableton Push 2 recording apparatus and my MacBook Pro and record songs in my car, but now that I look back, I really didn't record anything. I just connected everything and produced nothing worth listening too.

I'd look forward to seeing her reaction to the medicines, especially when it made her energetic afterwards. As I sat beside her recliner chair, I noticed she would get really cold, so we had to get her warm covers.

I couldn't get comfortable there, I'd be watching Mom as she slept, attempting to prepare myself wishing for the best. The doctor made sure I understood that her sickness was terminal, but my faith was with the Lord, and not man; because ultimately Jesus has the last say. We believed that.

One day once we were finished with the chemo appointment, and I drove home, the treatment was taking effect on mom's muscles and the ability to hold it. She cried out once I parked in our driveway to her daughter, my wife, EURDISE! who was her main caretaker aside from myself.

Mom had an accident on herself. My wife washed her, she had felt embarrassed. I could see her face as the door closed, gazing at me tearfully whimpering. It was the meds. One of the side effects was making her weak.

I Don't Know Why
She Was Proud Of Me

My Mother survived many strokes at once, and she needed therapy to regain her ability to walk again. My wife was by her side assisting her and coaching her as well as myself including a physical therapist that came three times a week. You got this Mommy. We all were trying to encourage her.

It was just like yesterday; I got married and my friend Arthur was there celebrating with us. Then next thing you know, Arthur was walking with a cane then he is dying from stomach cancer. R.I.P. Arthur L. Rutledge.

Mom wasn't in the mood for anything to eat. She had started to need assistance for stability walking up the stairs. I stood behind her step after step as she walked up one flight of stairs which had her gasping for air and eventually having to take breaks in between steps. Once she carried light grocery bags at her choosing just to help out.

My Mother and my wife would take turns buying groceries, and most of the time Mom would put her card up and buy us lunch and dinner. She loved getting sandwiches from Jersey Mike's and eating Panda Express (American Chinese food). But now she has no taste for it and no energy to feed herself, just a sip here and a bite there. She hardly drank anything. Her protein shakes water nothing. Her appearance did not suffer. She was a small woman overall and her skin stayed golden brown. No wrinkles although her locs hairstyle had disappeared.

I Don't Know Why
She Was Proud Of Me

One day my wife was doing her hair and as she attempted to brush and comb her hair, they detached from her head in sections. She cried and wept as my wife used my clippers to even out her remaining hair on her head.

I never liked to hear my Mother cry, but she was getting sicker, and she was seeing, and feeling, the effects of having this disease progress. I watched her live and grow. I cherished every moment we got to spend with one another.

I enjoyed the role reversal of her being under my care as I attempted to do the right thing by her. I pushed her in the wheelchair up and down ramps that led to the medical office where she got blood transfusions. I watched her love and triumph, but here I was watching her before my eyes. There was nothing I could do but pray and assist her until the point where the palliative care nurse and doctor informed me that they were there to make her comfortable at one point.

My wife and I had to adjust our lives dedicated to the wellbeing and healing of my Mommy Patricia Laverne Brown.

My wife, her angel, and I took turns on an open wound below her belly with bandages and swabs to clean the opening. My mom would lie there in sort of a baby form, but making sure the steps were done correctly, from hand washing, to gloves on during replacing the blood soaked gauze. But as months passed, she had gotten her appetite back.

We we're thinking about her moving to her room if she kept improving and getting stronger at this pace. One full hysterectomy later at age sixty-nine, was decided upon because the doctors felt that procedure would improve her quality of life moving forward. She felt she wouldn't need those lady parts anyway due to her age.

This was a procedure brought up by her team of doctors to remove the cancer. We had no idea that it had spread to the inner lining of her stomach, which caused her to have a bowel obstruction.

During this time, colorful lights illuminating through the neighborhood on a Christmas eve night. They glared not from a tree, but from an ambulance, and inside of it was Mommy. This was the last time I would see her being driven away never to return home alive.

So, I have a question for the readers, "Do you think I could've done more?"

If I could've saved her life, she would be proud of me. If I had been smart enough to make the right decisions on procedures the medical doctors could have performed, would she be proud of me?

After reading my story, do you know why she was proud of me? because I don't. I feel like Mom gave me something really sensitive to take care of, her life and I dropped the ball. Damn sometimes I feel like I messed everything up.

I'll miss the way Mom and I would sing Bill Withers "Lovely Day" or Earth Wind and Fire songs. She would also sing "Secret Garden" by Quincy Jones and friends. The funny thing is that I would do Barry White's part and Mom would do everyone else's part.

I'll miss her dancing to Curtis Mayfield and the Impressions "Check Out Your Mind." I used to think my Mother was a soul train dancer.

You must be careful what you do around children because they're watching.

I Don't Know Why She Was Proud Of Me

Outro to the Book in Lyrical Form

I could hear God calling

PATTY.

Uhhh

I could hear em calling

PATTY.

Uhhh PATTY!

Patricia Laverne Brown

Yeah

Patricia Laverne Brown.

Patty was savvy.

She'd gladly

Help if you're hurt badly.

But sadly, ovarian cancer took her from me.

In January, she made me happy.

Patty fell in love with a dude who couldn't stay out of jail. Hearing Bruno Mars made her jump up from her bed rails.

Patty had the brownskin that never wrinkled even on her death bed. It would twinkle when the sun hit it.

I Don't Know Why She Was Proud Of Me

I learned so much from Patty watching her chef in the kitchen.

Everything she told me I really tried to listen.

I was an only child, no sister no brother.

Her words echoed in one ear and came out the other. So much I saw the words.

I watched her party enjoying herself in a tenement structure. Till it was just her and I then life got tougher cause I had to watch beautiful mama suffer.

Could hear him calling PATTY. Uhhh PATTY!

Patricia Laverne Brown cleansed from the grime and had a good time spent growing up in Harlem between 7th and 8th up the block from Esplanade Garden - born in the early 50's with two brothers.

They were real men: Gerald D. Brown and Leslie, my uncles, may they rest in peace

Patricia Laverne Brown!

As she hung out with her friend Marlene playing skelly, she grew to her twenties, met a cat named Billy. He put one in her belly which was me.

A breached baby as she remained calm being a single mom. The struggle was real with dad being an ex-con.

Patty fell in love with a dude who couldn't stay out of jail.

The Good a.m. - by wmextra:

SUNDAY

Good a.m. Mommy, what a beautiful morning, birds chirping, squirrels jumping, sun shining, wheels turning.... Your mind....

Train on schedule, breakfast and lunch prepared.

People let's go give the Lord a praise he's the producer of all this marvel.

MONDAY

Good a.m. Mommy so it's the first Monday of April a new batch of days to give praise, a new morning to rise and shine, a new morning to understand that everything is in God's will whether it feels unfair or rewarding. Life is hard but work towards a good one. Have a great start of the day, back to business party over.

Last week was incredibly challenging for me and I know some of you faced challenges too ... be safe and thank God for the gift of life and fellowship.

* * *

Good a.m. Mommy. It's a grey Monday. It's raining. My favorite is coming off an Allstar weekend of no complaints and birthday celebrations. My mom turned 65 yesterday. My son is 21 today ... why not it's March. He's a Pisces. I thank God for his mercies amongst my family friends, co-workers, and children. Keep it moving there's work to do

TUESDAY

Good a.m. Mommy we are so fortunate to awake this morning ... a chance to do it all again ... a chance to gain victory ... a better understanding of why we do what we do.... We bring light to dark environments we bring <u>smiles vs frowns</u> because we know through it all he is with us and without that blessing we would dwell within the darkness and welcome people with frowns and unhappy gestures.... I know that blessings are spiritual not monetary or having things. It's being alive in the spirit and spreading this understanding that this Tuesday will be better than Monday.

* * *

Good a.m. Mommy have a wonderful day stay productive and focus on being the light that people need and mask your own situation with the grace that allows you to say Good a.m. Have a wonderful day even if nobody responds.... Good Tuesday y'all, watch it unfurl.

Good a.m. Mommy, same grind, different blessing, Love you guys, be strong. The enemy does not want you to rebuild your temple to its fullest potential. He wants you to destroy it and have you stuck in unbelief and stupor for the façade of chaos and sorrow.... Been there

The Good a.m. - by wmextra:

done that.... Not my comfort zone. I'm *gonna* put on my Tuesday smile and keep it moving for the experienced ones. Hallelujah!

* * *

Good a.m. Mommy today is a special Tuesday. Today marks the official quarterly change point in 2016. What I mean is if you haven't begun to change and enhance parts of us already, start now ... this year can't move on without support from one another.

WEDNESDAY

I'm moving forward readjusting constantly, readapting to my surroundings, continuing to chisel through walls of miscommunication, insult, sadness with a praise and a nail of worship and the strength of hallelujah now that's a breakthrough and in due season people will see the light you could tell.... Good a.m. It's Wednesday

THURSDAY

Good a.m. Mommy, to a great feeling ... a Thursday brothers and sisters. Today is a day of promise for us to be the best we can be. Today is a day for my morning people to awake and have a positive outlook on our country, communities, and families as my song says, I love you and you and all of you.

* * *

Good a.m. Mommy, can you feel transformation? If you don't make an effort to do something different for the good, then you won't feel the change for the better. I can feel the effects of a lil exercise routine, a diet, taking a lil more time to think when making decisions.... I consult with my wife before I act.... I'm a mess but God is working on me. Have a good Friday eve.

FRIDAY

Good a.m. Mommy Happy Friday, what a week.... The blessing continues.... Communication is the key.

I got this bible in my bookbag I plan on communicating....

New day, and

New pathway.

While I was driving to the train station today, I was listening to the radio and there was a tune that stuck in my head. It went like this ... you're a good father, it's who you are it's who you are ... you're a good father, it's who you are.

The Good a.m. - by wmextra:

Thank you, Lord, for waking me up this morning and renewing my life erasing my sorrows and woes.... Safe passages y'all

SATURDAY

Good a.m. Mommy ahhhh Saturday. Some people actually spend all week being productive, professional, courteous, creative, and pumped to get to this moment.

Thank you, Lord for waking me up this a.m. Bless our family, friends, co-workers, and children with safe passage from point A to point B and C and thereafter.... Enjoy your day. Saturdays are the best.

* * *

Good a.m. Folks, what a weekend of love, the unexpected, and blessing you know there was Superman vs. Batman - love vs. hate - good vs. evil and the enemy vs. God's people. Don't let anyone steal your joy you know this ... today! 2mm and thereafter. I was so busy this weekend. I hope it went well for you.

Redweek at the Church Poem

This week has been filled with a lot of emotion for me. I've seen a lot of good and a lot of bad within this Redweek. I've seen a lot of victories and a lot of determination to try again. I've seen a lot of hard work paying off, and as always, a lot of destruction, mayhem, and chaos. When one door closes another one opens. There are some that doubt the power of Jesus Christ. I don't and I know that it is he who builds me up, delivers me and has me singing today Happy Friday.

Poem for Mommy's Granddaughter's Boyfriend

Good a.m. Malik words can't describe how much I value you as a person in this world continue to make decisions to better yourself and help others where you see fit. Alysha mostly, she needs a man like you in her life … at the end of the day you're the man. Stay strong for your grandparents, your mom, sister … etc. 2015 … Move forward.

From the Desk of William Brown

Mmmm...mmmmm I'm feeling the Spirit. A new thing is being created. A new mission has started. A new day has been recorded. A new mindset has been provided. Old things will be updated.

My daughter is turning 30. She said I should turn up for her!!!!

My sons will learn new energy and absorb all the history from our ancestors to provide a better future.... Celebration is on cue and on deck.

I couldn't do it without y'all. We appreciate all the love and support. We thank God for everything. He's in our Cousins, Aunties, Nieces, Nephews, Daddy, Mommy, Grandmas, Grandpas, Friends, Associates, Coworkers, Uncles, Step Mommy, Step Father, and even Pastors.

I DONT KNOW

WHY SHE WAS

PROUD OF ME

BIOGRAPHY

William Brown has been married for thirteen years to Eurdise and a father of six, three boys and three girls.

Brown was raised in Harlem, an African-American heritage, known for its intimate jazz clubs. He could feel the vibe and went in the direction of HipHop.

He has another name William Extra, also known as KNGAMPRCK, is a recording artist from 145th Street in Harlem, New York City. He has been self-training himself for nearly two decades to utilize the Ableton Live Daw to craft his signature sound. He has been working on his clothing line Frank Vilain aka F.VLN which has a grand effect on its admirers and clients throughout the greater tri-state area and abroad.

William Extra has been featured on the legendary D.J. Ron-G mixtapes when mixtapes were physical cassettes. He made his debut on New York City's own Prop Master Kool D.J. Red Alert's Presents album in 1997 and had a year-long promo push on the New York radio station Hot 97 with a compliment from media mogul Wendy Williams.

He was also featured on the legendary rap group from Harlem Mobstyle's album The Game of Death.

William Extra is also the president of his own record label 1HUN4ORTY5IFST Recordings. He debut memoir is this book titled, "I Don't Know Why She Was Proud of Me," which recalls his upbringing and being raised by his mother and witnessing her untimely death from ovarian cancer reflecting their times together.

www.ingramcontent.com/pod-product-compliance
Lightning Source LLC
LaVergne TN
LVHW061547070526
838199LV00077B/6937